THE AUTHORS

John Silvester has been a crime reporter in Melbourne since 1978. He worked for *The Sunday Times* 'Insight' team in London in 1990, and has co-authored several crime books, including the best-seller *Underbelly*. He is currently senior crime writer for *The Age*.

Andrew Rule has been a journalist since 1975 and has worked in newspapers, television and radio. He wrote *Cuckoo*, the true story of the notorious 'Mr Stinky' case, and has edited and published several other books, including the original *Underbelly*.

They won the prestigious Ned Kelly Award for True Crime writing for *Underbelly 3*.

UNDER BELLY 9

MORE TRUE CRIME STORIES

by JOHN SILVESTER and ANDREW RULE

Published in Australia by
Floradale Productions Pty Ltd and Sly Ink Pty Ltd
October 2005

Distributed wholesale by
Gary Allen Pty Ltd,
9 Cooper Street,
Smithfield, NSW
Telephone 02 9725 2933

Underbelly 9
More True Crime Stories

ISBN – 0 9752318 7 1

Cover photograph by James Braund
jamesbraund@bigpond.com

'The infectiousness
of crime is like
that of the plague

Napoleon Bonaparte

DEDICATION

To Deputy Commissioner
John Carl Mengler (retired),
who fought crime for
decades without becoming
infected by what he saw.
And to his wonderful wife
Heather who passed away
on December 31, 2004.

CONTENTS

> If it was anyone else in my position, they'd get a key to the city. It's just unfortunate that it's me.

1.
THE MAN WHO WOULDN'T BLINK

MICK GATTO has made a career out of grabbing his chances as they have come along. From boxer to enforcer to the more sophisticated title 'industrial mediator', Gatto has methodically crafted a reputation as a man who can persuade others to see his point of view. In some ways the reputation has grown bigger than the reality.

Media reports suggest the Melbourne identity first came to prominence as a boxer who was close to winning the national heavyweight title. Some even say he won fifteen fights by knockout. This says a lot about sports reporting in general, boxing coverage in particular.

The truth, always elusive at ringside, is that as a heavyweight boxer Mick Gatto was never going to be a genuine headliner. But he would make page one much later for actions more violent than ever could be found inside the square ring. He was tough, with a knockout punch and a big heart, but too slow to make the big time and too bright to allow himself to become another punching bag for young, faster fighters.

Gatto's official record is modest. Over seven years he fought under Queensberry rules just nine times. The records do not record what happened in the streets. In 1973 he had five bouts, losing one when Mark Ecimovic – a boxer who later fought for the Australian heavyweight crown – knocked him out in the first round.

The following year he fought twice, losing once on points and winning the other by knockout. Strictly a preliminary fighter, he did little for three years until a main event on the then popular *TV Ringside* threatened to fall over when one of the boxers withdrew.

Enter Big Mick, who entertained the crowd by going the distance in a ten-round fight with Reno Zurek – later to be crowned NSW heavyweight champion. Two years later he again fought Zurek, this time in Griffith in an eight-rounder. Again Mick lost on points but went the distance. It was Gatto's last big fight, but he was the main event.

Mick Gatto learned much in his journeyman boxing years. He learned that if you are wounded never let your opponent know you are hurt. He learned that when cornered it is best to cover up. He learned that the clinch can be the boxer's best friend because when you are holding an opponent he can do less damage than if he has room to swing. He saw that big fights are rarely won with one punch and good boxers don't fight out of anger or fear. They do their homework and anticipate their opponent's likely moves. In seconds they can calculate the risks and rewards of every option and choose their moment to launch an attack. Hotheads get the crowds cheering but it is the cool ones who more often take home the purse. Unless, of course, the fight is fixed.

Gatto knew that local boys win more than their fair share and given the chance you should fight on your home turf with trusted friends in your corner. He also learned that the men who are truly feared and respected – from lightweights to heavyweights – have one thing in common. When faced with danger they never blink.

MORE than 25 years after leaving the ring Gatto would enter another gladiatorial arena where there could only be one winner – the Supreme Court of Victoria – to face the charge of murdering a notorious hitman named Andrew Veniamin. For several years Melbourne – a sprawling suburbia with a low crime rate, a respected police force and a tendency towards self-congratulation – had been the centre of a vicious, and unusually public underworld war.

Colourful men with strange nicknames, no jobs and unexplained wealth were turning up dead. A man like Nik 'The Bulgarian' Radev – a refugee who hadn't held a legitimate job for twenty years yet managed to maintain a five-star lifestyle – was typical of the victims.

Virtually unknown until his very public murder, Radev was shot next to his luxury Mercedes in Coburg in April 2003. Shortly before his execution he had paid a dentist $55,000 to whiten and crown his teeth, turning them from basic Bulgarian to glitzy Hollywood. It was a waste of money: he was shot up to seven times in the head and body. Fittingly, he was later buried in a $30,000 gold casket with what was left of his million-dollar smile.

Another victim, Mark Moran, was shot dead outside his $1.3million home. Moran was ostensibly an unemployed pastry chef. Usually Melbourne's main players in the criminal world watched the flashy ones like Radev come in full-on and go out feet first. But this time it was different.

First, the war was public and embarrassing. The police force, which had long fancied itself the best in the country, was beginning to look silly. Indeed, Assistant Commissioner (crime) Simon Overland would later admit police had dropped the ball in investigating organised crime. This meant – as police hate to look silly – there would be a major reaction: they would form a task force called *Purana*, and it would prove to be more effective than many thought possible. The task force would crack the gangland code of silence and charge 51 people with almost 200 offences. Thirteen suspects were eventually charged over six alleged murders, seven with conspiracy to incite murder, six over guns and 25 with drug-related offences.

The government was also made to look silly and politicians who are seen as soft on crime can imagine themselves losing their seats when voters get their chance at the polls. So the government gave police new powers to call suspects to secret hearings, and seize assets that may have taken years to hide. All of this was extremely bad for business for men who had already learned the ropes.

It had long been a standing joke that for decades Gatto had spent a fortune on flowers and death notices as friends and foes lost their lives in violent circumstances. Some cynics suggest he had the death notice number of the *Herald Sun* classifieds on speed dial, often ringing before the latest victim's name had been made public. In the early 1970s and '80s he paid his respects as gangsters such as brothers Brian and Les Kane were gunned down. But by the 1990s many of his own network were targeted.

Alphonse John Gangitano was a close associate of Gatto's

and police often saw them together. Both were young members of a group known by police as the Carlton Crew. Of Italian origin but raised in Australia, they had some of the mannerisms of the so-called mafia but would spend their Saturdays like many other Aussies, sipping a drink, watching the races and having a punt. When invited to the Collingwood President's Room at Victoria Park, Gatto spent more time out the back watching the horse races on television than the football in front of him. Gatto and Gangitano both had an interest in Italian food, imported suits, gambling and boxing. In fact Alphonse was a fight promoter and boxing manager for a short time although his form of negotiating deals bordered on the eccentric. Heavily in the camp of local boxer Lester Ellis, he once attacked, bashed and bit champion Barry Michael – an Ellis rival – in a city nightclub in 1987. Even a shark like Don King didn't chew on his opponents. He left that to Mike Tyson inside the ring.

While Gatto and Gangitano were friends they were not as close as many thought. Gangitano liked his reputation as the Black Prince of Lygon Street and spend a decade in the headlines. Gatto preferred to remain out of the glare of media attention. Gangitano was the show pony, Gatto the stayer. Repeated police investigations found that while Gangitano was a professional criminal he did not have the asset base to justify his reputation as a Mr Big. More style than substance, they believed. But that didn't mean he wasn't dangerous.

ON February 6, 1995, Gangitano was at party in Wando Grove, East St Kilda, held to raise bail for a man charged with armed robbery. Not exactly the Salvation Army but it is the thought that counts. The underworld charity bash was not tax deductible but that would not have concerned those present as most didn't bother to pay tax on their largely undisclosed earnings.

At 4.40am, Gangitano went outside with another colourful Melbourne identity, Gregory John Workman. There was an argument and Gangitano did not like to lose arguments. Workman was shot seven times in the back and once in the chest, which meant he lost both the debate and his life. Gangitano was charged with murder but persuaded two key female witnesses to change their stories and then generously rewarded them with extended overseas vacations. The case against Gangitano then collapsed. But the big man with the bigger reputation didn't take his second chance and continued to participate in high-profile criminal activities until his violent death. He was shot dead inside his Templestowe home on January 16, 1998.

Present, but not involved in the shooting of Gangitano was Graham 'The Munster' Kinniburgh – a man who was a father figure to Mick Gatto. The shooter was said to be Jason Moran, who would himself later join the list of gangland murder victims.

Some say Gatto and Gangitano had grown apart in the years before the shooting. Alphonse drew the attention of the media and police to business matters that people like Gatto felt were best left in private. However, in a rare interview, Gatto said later they were still friends at the time of the murder but he had grown tired of his name always being linked to the dead gangster. 'Why can't they let him rest in peace?'

LIKE Gangitano, Mick Gatto did not hanker for a nine to five job. He has been described over the years as a standover man – a claim he hotly denies – a landscape gardener, a professional punter and a gambling identity connected to Melbourne's once profitable and illegal two-up school. These days he is a consultant for the building industry – a highly paid problem solver. He also has an interest in industrial cranes. He has convictions for burglary, assaulting police, possessing firearms, and obtaining financial advantage by deception. He was also charged with extortion, blackmail and making threats to kill but these annoying matters were struck out at committal.

Big Mick says such immature behaviour is all in the past. He maintains that these days he is, as they say, straight as a gun barrel.

In February 2002, he was invited via a subpoena to appear at the royal commission into the building industry to discuss his growing role as an industrial relations consultant on Melbourne building sites. The commission was interested in an alleged payment of $250,000 to solve some sticky industrial problems for a company that understandably did not want extended labour conflicts. Inquiring minds at the commission found that $189,750 was paid to a company controlled by Mick Gatto and his business partner and good friend, Dave 'The Rock' Hedgcock.

When he gave evidence Gatto appeared offended that people could suggest he used threats of violence to solve problems. 'I'm not a standover man. I'm not a man of ill repute. Fair enough I've got a chequered past ... but I paid for ... whatever I have done wrong.'

Police who know Gatto say he is unfailingly courteous, slow to anger and always in control. He uses body language to ensure that people around him are aware that he remains a physically imposing man. 'It is not so much what he says but what he leaves unsaid,' one detective said.

His unofficial office was La Porcella, a large Italian restaurant on the corner of Faraday and Rathdowne Streets, Carlton. Most weekdays he could be found there, often in the company of those he respected – men with healthy appetites and colourful pasts. But he was rarely there at weekends. That was time for the family, he said. It is said that people with problems were prepared to pay $5000 to sit at the table with Mick and discuss solutions. Sometimes he could help and other times he couldn't. But it would always be a pleasant and entertaining luncheon.

Many police and criminals dine out on Gatto stories and it is often impossible to distil reality from myth because those close to the big man remain staunchly loyal and staunchly silent. Those not so close seem to believe it would not be wise to tell tales out of the old school.

But there are several stories to indicate that while Gatto is charming and does not use violence indiscriminately, he succeeds because people fear the consequences of not seeing his point of view. In one case he was able to jolt the memory of a businessman who owed an associate $75,000.

The debt was paid and Gatto was said to have kept $25,000 as his commission. Everyone was a winner. The man who owed the money is still able to walk without a limp, the businessman did not have to write off the sum as a bad debt and Mick was handsomely paid for two phone calls.

One solicitor once used Gatto's name to threaten someone who owed him $15,000 and then asked Big Mick to collect the debt. A policeman said Gatto did as he was asked but pocketed the full amount as a fine for the lawyer using his name without permission. Again everyone was a winner – one man learned to pay his debts, another not to use people's names to make idle threats and Mick's bank balance received a healthy injection. Another detective said he knew of case of a man who was dancing at a nightclub when he had a nail punched into his shoulder. The reason? He owed Gatto $400.

Yet another policeman said he believed Gatto once shot a man in the leg in Carlton. When police tried to get a statement from the victim, the man not only denied that he knew who had shot him but denied he had been shot at all. When asked why he was sitting in casualty with blood seeping from the wound, he said he didn't know why his leg was leaking.

Another time a man came asking for help but Mick's advice was to deal with the matter rather than employ others who might lack the subtlety to solve the problem. This was not a time for the use of a sledgehammer to crack a walnut – or in this case two walnuts. Years later the man could see the wisdom of the advice. Many police had a grudging respect for Gatto as a man who did not go looking for trouble and saw him as 'old school'.

But the underworld landscape was changing and Melbourne's criminal establishment was being drawn into a gangland war not entirely of their making. A man was shot in the stomach as a warning over an alleged drug debt. But the victim was not intimidated into doing nothing – in fact, his desire for revenge is thought to have been the catalyst for a violent feud that would cost several lives and change the criminal justice system in Victoria. Some men close to Gatto were to be victims – Mark Moran in June 2000, his half-brother Jason Moran, shot with his friend Pasquale Barbaro in June 2003. Later Jason Moran's father, Lewis, shot in March 2004.

In each case, Gatto responded with his usual death notices and sympathy cards but it was the murder of Graham 'The Munster' Kinniburgh that hit him the hardest.

Kinniburgh was shot dead outside his Kew home on December 13, 2003. He had begun to carry a gun for the first time in years after hearing he may have been on the hit list, but it didn't help. He was ambushed as he was about to walk up his driveway with some late night shopping.

The death of an old and respected friend distressed Gatto and made him realise that the dominoes around him were falling and he could be next. Within hours of the murder the dogs were barking (wrongly as it turned out) that one of the men who killed 'The Munster' was a hot-headed street criminal turned hit man called Andrew 'Benji' Veniamin.

VENIAMIN was a small man with a growing reputation for ruthless violence. Like Mick Gatto he was a former boxer, although they were from different eras – and vastly different ends of the weight divisions. Any chances of Veniamin making a name as a boxer ended when at nineteen he badly broke his leg and damaged his knee in a motorbike accident. But all this meant was that he could channel his violent inclinations to activities outside the ring.

Heavily tattooed, with a close-cropped haircut and a bullet-shaped head, the brooding Veniamin looked like a man who could take offence easily and was only a glance away from yet another over-reaction.

According to *Purana* task force investigators, Veniamin's criminal career could be broken into three phases. In the beginning he was a street thug in Melbourne's west. He ran with two other would-be gangsters, old schoolmates Paul Kallipolitis and Dino Dibra, and specialised in run-throughs, ripping off and robbing drug dealers who grew hydroponic marijuana crops in rented houses.

Veniamin had a criminal record that began in 1992 with a $50 fine for the theft of a motor car. In 1993, he was convicted of intentionally or recklessly causing injury and sentenced to 200 hours of unpaid community work. Over the next decade he was found guilty of theft, robbery, false imprisonment, assaulting police, arson, deception and threatening to cause serious injury.

The nature of the modern underworld is that access to drugs

– and drug money – means relatively minor players can become influential figures in a matter of months.

While Gatto was known as a man who always looked for amicable solutions, Veniamin was a hot-head who saw violence as the first resort. Pasquale Zaffina was an old friend of Veniamin but that didn't stop the gangster trying to move in on his girlfriend. When Zaffina objected, Veniamin responded with a surprising lack of contrition. He fired shots into Zaffina's parents' house and, apparently unimpressed with the results, left a bomb at the residence and threatened to kill Zaffina's sister.

To settle matters they agreed to meet for a fight in a park in Melbourne's western suburbs with seconds to back them up – as though conducting an old-fashioned duel. They agreed it would be fists and no guns. But as they shaped up, Veniamin produced a .38 calibre handgun and aimed it at Zaffina, who managed to push the gun towards the ground. Three shots hit him in the leg but he lived to tell the story – at Gatto's trial, as it would turn out.

The defence would make much of the Zaffina story, claiming it showed Veniamin could conceal a .38, would ambush and attempt to kill people and did not care if witnesses were present. But that would be much later.

By 2002 Veniamin saw himself as a man of substance (as well as substances) and felt he could associate with men with established reputations. These included members of the so-called Carlton Crew and Mick Gatto in particular.

The younger gun exhibited all the signs of being starstruck and appeared to hero worship the man who was a household name in a certain type of household.

Gatto saw Veniamin as dangerous but extended his big hand of friendship, working on the principle that you keep your friends close and your enemies closer. He knew the new boy was vicious but Veniamin was a man of growing power in the west and Gatto thought that if he needed muscle in the Sunshine area 'Benji' could be handy.

Gatto loved to build networks – some good, some bad. Veniamin – twenty years younger – was high maintenance and at times was only just tolerated by the Carlton blue bloods. He was said to have asked Gatto to provide him with firearms and on more than one occasion the older man had to intervene after Veniamin involved himself in mindless violence at nightclubs.

Gatto said in evidence, 'Well, I remember just one occasion, that he asked me if I could get guns for him, revolvers and, you know, I said I'd ask, but I mean I had no intention of doing that, to be honest, because it's a no-win situation. And the other occasion I can't really remember, but he was forever getting himself into trouble at nightclubs and what have you, and I was always sort of getting involved, sort of patching things up.'

But Veniamin was more than just a camp follower. He was already a killer. Police now believe he pulled the trigger in at least four murders and had direct knowledge of others.

FRANK Benvenuto was the son of Liborio Benvenuto, the former Godfather of the mafia-like crime group the Honoured Society, who died of natural causes in 1988. Frank was still seen as a man of influence and was a good friend of the notorious gunman Victor George Peirce, but by 2000 he was said to be in debt to drug dealers. He was shot dead outside his Beaumaris home on May 8, 2000.

Police believe Veniamin was the killer. They also say he was the gunman who killed his former friends and criminal associates – Dino Dibra, who was shot dead near his West Sunshine home on October 14, 2000, and Paul Kallipolitis, whose body was found in his West Sunshine home on October 25, 2002. Veniamin was the main suspect in the murder of standover man Nik Radev, who was shot dead on April 15, 2003. Radev had an appointment to see Veniamin on the morning he was murdered.

But in 2003, Veniamin's allegiances changed. He swapped camps, moving to become the bodyguard and close friend of a man who was said to have declared war on the crime world's old guard. A drug dispute and a shooting are believed to have led a group of little-known criminals to plot to destroy the criminal establishment.

The story goes that a high-profile drug dealer was bashed in Lygon Street by a Perth bikie. Gatto was said to have been present and done nothing to protect the Melbourne dealer, believing it was none of his business. Veniamin drove the badly-injured man to hospital and was then persuaded to change sides. That is one version. There are others. But for whatever reason Veniamin became the constant companion of a man who was said to be organising the extermination of Melbourne's best-known colourful characters. Mick Gatto was one of the men thought to be at risk of being gunned down.

Weeks after the Radev shooting, police established the *Purana* task force. The task force called for all intelligence holdings on suspects such as Veniamin and was stunned to find how little was known about the vicious killer. Assistant Commissioner (crime) Simon Overland would later use Veniamin as an example of how police had failed to monitor organised crime in Victoria.

Police approached Veniamin in 2003 with a message to 'pull up' – warning him his activities meant he was now also a potential victim. It was not an empty statement as to this point at least five shooters in Melbourne's gangland war had already become murder victims. When detectives told him he was likely to die violently, Benji didn't seem fazed. He told them he was well aware of the risks and had already told his parents that if he was killed they should honour the underworld code of silence and refuse to co-operate with police. He wrote to one of the authors suggesting publicity at such a delicate time could 'endanger my life'.

Having changed camps, Benji became blindly loyal to the drug dealer who police believed wanted to kill all his perceived enemies. But there were certain perks in becoming a family friend and constant bodyguard to the new breed gangster. He was invited to share a family holiday with the man, staying in a five-star resort in Queensland. It was a case of the boy from Sunshine spending up big in the Sunshine State. Never the master of measuring risks, he took to dog paddling in the surf even though he could hardly swim. By late 2003 he had moved into a city penthouse and drove a borrowed $200,000 car. Yet he was still registered to pick up the dole.

Veniamin was one of the first principal targets of the *Purana* task force and police developed a strategy of trying to harass and disrupt his routine so he would not have the freedom to continue to kill. *Purana* investigator Boris Buick gave evidence at the Gatto trial that police were constantly pulling Veniamin over on the road and raiding his home and those of his friends and relatives. He said this curtailed his criminal activities:

To the best of my knowledge, and as I said, we had saturated coverage of him, he was no longer committing acts of violence and was well aware of our interest in him. As well as essentially saturating the deceased by means of surveillance, personal surveillance and electronic surveillance, we also commenced regularly intercepting him and his associates, specifically seeking to disrupt their criminal activities.

We searched vehicles and other persons, of associates of his, and some other premises that he was associated with. And he was well aware at that stage, and we essentially made it aware to him that we were targeting him and his associates ... to prevent further offending, in particular to prevent offences of a violent nature and involving firearms.

Police bugged his home and car and had a court order to bug his telephones. The court order covered the period from July 20, 2003, to May 19, 2004 – coincidentally just four days before he was killed. Veniamin knew he was bugged and complained to Gatto that anyone he spoke to was raided a short time later. But the constant police surveillance helped clear him in at least one case. When Graeme Kinniburgh was shot dead, police were quickly able to establish Benji was near Taylors Lakes at the time – on the opposite side of Melbourne from the murder scene in Kew.

Veniamin loved guns and was always trying to find more, allegedly keeping one cache of weapons at a friendly kebab shop. But with police always near him, he could not always carry a weapon. According to *Purana* investigator Detective Senior Constable Stephen Baird (who was to die suddenly just months after the trial): *Veniamin became paranoid, in fact, about being surveilled by police, both physical and electronic, and also paranoid about being intercepted by police at any time and both his person searched and any vehicle he was being in searched for firearms.* So why then did he carry a .38 revolver with him to meet Mick Gatto in a Carlton restaurant on March 23, 2004?

ON December 22, 2003, nine days after Graham Kinniburgh's murder, Gatto met Veniamin and others at the Crown Casino in what police claim was an attempted peace conference. For police it was an ideal spot as the area was saturated with security cameras and the meeting could be monitored. For the main players, who did not trust each other, it was also an ideal place for the meeting. It was neutral ground and the cameras ensured there could be no ambush. The Atrium Bar at Crown is a world away from a dead-end corridor at the back of a Carlton restaurant.

The cameras even picked up the jockey-sized Veniamin kissing the much larger Gatto with the traditional mafia-style peck on the cheek as a respectful welcome.

Detectives later employed a lip-reader to discover what the suspects said. According to the lip-reader, Gatto chatted to a man loosely connected to Veniamin – a man suspected of organising Kinniburgh's murder.

He said, 'It's not my war. You walk away from this and mind your own business. If someone comes up to you for that sort of shit, if someone comes up to me with the same sort of shit I'll do the same thing. I'll be careful with you. You be careful with me. I believe you. You believe me. Now we're even.'

And walk away they did. But no-one was even. Gatto could only have concluded that it was not a matter of if, only when, there would be an attempt on his life.

The nature of his phone calls to Veniamin changed. The prosecution argued that telephone intercepts showed 'a growing menace in Gatto's voice' that Veniamin failed to pick up. Gatto later argued his phone conversations were never threatening. 'I just wanted to know what he was doing, what he was up to, and you know, keep your friends close and your enemies closer, you know. It was that sort of thing.'

On December 29 Gatto saw two men drive near his house. The passenger, he said, was a dead ringer for Veniamin. And more disturbingly, the passenger ducked down when Gatto looked in his direction. The next day he rang Benji and was relieved when he found he was in Port Douglas rather than Doncaster.

Police telephone intercepts showed that Gatto and Veniamin spoke regularly, often referring to each other as 'buddy' and 'champ'. An example was a call from Veniamin to Gatto on Friday, March 19 – the last day Benji's phones were tapped.

Veniamin: *What's doin', buddy?*

Gatto says he hasn't heard from him in a month and Veniamin replies: *You know, I swear to you, mate, every bloke I've rung off this phone has been raided.*

Veniamin tells Gatto: *Mate, I'm still there, mate.*

Gatto: *Well, mate, that's assuring. I fuckin' hope you're here a long time, buddy.* As Gatto probably was not overly concerned with Veniamin's long-term health it is likely the comment was laced with irony and possibly even menace.

Veniamin, always a literal type, either ignores or is unaware of the subtext: *I've been meaning to drop into that … that joint where you're there.*

Gatto: *Mate, I'm there every day, buddy. Every day we're there.*

Veniamin: *I promise you, mate, I swear to you, I'm gonna come. I want to come.*

Gatto: *Mate, any time you want to, buddy, you know where we are.*

Veniamin, who has only days earlier been released from hospital after an attack of pancreatitis says: *I've just been a bit stressed, I've been in and out of hospital the last two weeks, you know.*

Gatto: *I heard, mate, I heard.* He adds: *Mate, stay quiet, buddy.*

Veniamin: *Oh mate, I am, mate.*

Gatto: *Stay quiet.*

Veniamin: *But I'm still there, mate.*
Gatto: *Yeah.*
Veniamin: *Don't forget.*
Gatto: *I know that. I know. All right.*
Veniamin: *All right, buddy.*
Gatto: *Take care of yourself, mate, keep in touch.*
Veniamin: *I'll drop in there.*
Gatto: *You're welcome any time, mate.*
Veniamin: *Thanks very much, buddy.*
Gatto: *Take care, Andrew.*
Veniamin: *See you, buddy. Bye, mate.*
Gatto: *See you, mate, thanks.*

Police would ask later whether the 'Stay quiet, buddy' comment was well-meaning advice or a veiled threat. Certainly it is unlikely that Veniamin would have considered that when he said 'I'm still there, mate' that four days later he wouldn't be.

On March 23, Gatto rang Veniamin's mobile phone and asked him to come to the restaurant. It was about 2pm. What detectives can establish is that Veniamin was in the Melbourne Magistrates' Court that morning and that when he received the phone call he was in his borrowed silver Mercedes that was bugged by police. A few minutes later he called someone else and said he was about to 'catch up with someone ... the big bloke'. He double-parked the car and walked into the restaurant and sat with Gatto and others at a raised table. Both were in their trademark attire – Gatto was wearing a suit, Veniamin a T-shirt and track pants.

Later he and Gatto walked to the back of the restaurant and entered a dead end corridor for a private chat. One side of the corridor running to the fridge was stacked with cartons of tinned tomatoes. The width was just wide enough for the shoulders of the former heavyweight. Gatto had handed his mobile phone to his friend Ron Bongetti and Veniamin left the keys to his car on the table.

Next moment five shots were fired and Gatto walked out leaving Veniamin dead on the floor. Three shots hit Veniamin at point blank range. One smashed the main artery in his neck, the second severed his spinal cord and the third entered his head near the right ear. There were powder burns on Gatto's suit showing the two men were next to each other when the shots were fired, the gun virtually pressed against the victim. Gatto later had short-term hearing problems from the shots and thought he may have been nicked on the left ear by one of the bullets.

Police were called and a remarkably calm Gatto explained to them that it was self-defence – that Veniamin had drawn a gun and in the struggle the smaller man was shot. 'He pulled a gun out … he pulled out a gun and he tried to shoot me and he finished second best,' he told police at the scene. Gatto was taken back to the homicide squad offices in St Kilda Road, given a legal caution and told he could have access to a solicitor. He didn't need to be told he needed legal representation. He had phoned a solicitor from the restaurant – and he didn't need to check the Yellow Pages for the number.

He was swabbed for gunshot residue and later for DNA. Around 11pm a short formal interview began. Mr Gatto said: 'I've had some legal advice and I just wish to say that I've done nothing wrong and I've acted in complete self-defence, and I'd like to make no further comment at this stage.'

Purana investigator Boris Buick asked: 'Is that the extent of the statement that you wish to make?' Gatto said: 'That's it.' Police were faced with a dilemma. They had one very brief version of events – Gatto's self-defence argument.

The case for murder was weak and relied exclusively on

circumstantial evidence. But what if police had freed Gatto and allowed the matter to go to inquest at the Coroner's Court? There would have been allegations that because Veniamin was out of control and because police lacked the evidence to charge him with the four murders he was suspected of, they had 'green-lighted' Gatto to kill him. It would have been hard to explain how the warrant to bug Veniamin's telephones lapsed just four days before he was killed. And there were issues worth exploring in front of a Supreme Court jury.

Why did Gatto, a self-described industrial mediator, have a body bag in the boot of his Mercedes outside the restaurant? If Veniamin planned to murder Gatto, why would he do it in a restaurant filled with Gatto's friends, almost guaranteeing retribution? Why kill a man in a place frequented by police and often under surveillance? Veniamin was unaware his phone was no longer bugged and would have believed police had recorded that last conversation with Gatto before he arrived. If it was a planned hit he had virtually no chance of fabricating an alibi. Why did he leave his keys on the table, meaning he would have to return to confront the rest of Gatto's team before he could escape? Veniamin had stopped carrying guns because police had repeatedly raided him in the previous year. He had been in court and unarmed that morning. When and where did he get the .38 before his meeting with Gatto? Why did he choose a tiny corridor for the confrontation where the much bigger and stronger Gatto could so easily overpower him?

There were many theories, including one that Gatto, using the lessons learned in the ring, chose a moment when there were no witnesses to counterattack. There was a feeling that Gatto was too proud to sneak in the dark to ambush an enemy or pay others to do his dirty work.

Another theory was that such a public killing was a statement to others that if the war was to continue he would come after them. Or did Veniamin, increasingly erratic and more drug-dependent, just lose it, as he had before? Did he react in a way he would not live to regret? Was it, as Gatto has always maintained, a clear-cut case of self-defence?

Certainly, those close to Veniamin had trouble with the self-defence theory. The day after his funeral, Lewis Moran, an old-school criminal and friend of Gatto, was shot dead in the Brunswick Club in what police believe was a direct payback.

IT would take more than a year for the trial to begin and it was a very different Mick Gatto who arrived in court from solitary confinement. Unable to eat in restaurants, he had embarked on a fitness campaign, shadow boxing for hours in his cell. He had lost 30 kilos and was back to his fighting weight. The Supreme Court can diminish a man. Men with reputations as tough guys tend to appear intimidated in the dock. They must look up to the judge, bow when he enters and wonder about the twelve strangers who will decide their fate. They are led in and out by prison guards and those who are aggressive soon learn to at least behave passively.

But Mick Gatto did not appear diminished by the experience. Well dressed, he seemed at home in the combative environment and far from intimidated. He was back on the balls of his feet. During breaks when the jury was not present he would wander to the back of the court to talk to friends and family who attended. It was almost like a royal walk as he chatted to his subjects.

He would talk to reporters and compliment them if he thought their coverage was a fair representation of the evidence so far, evidence that would decide his future. Mick Gatto was 49. If found guilty of a gangland murder he would be looking at about sixteen years minimum prison sentence. If that happened, he would be 65 when released and yesterday's man.

Robert Richter QC is used to representing the big guns, from business mogul turned cartoon caricature John Elliott to fallen funny man Steve Vizard – those who can afford the best often turn to the veteran Melbourne barrister. Regardless if the alleged offences are indiscretions in the boardroom or gangland killings, Richter's advice tends to be the same.

In court he is the boss and the client is just there for the ride. He believes that patients don't tell surgeons how to operate and clients shouldn't try to run complex criminal trials. When it comes to murder he is of the view that in nearly every case the accused is better off letting the defence lawyers do the talking. Sit up straight and look attentive, engage the jury without intimidating them, don't look bored and don't look angry. And, most importantly, shut up.

As with most defence lawyers, his strategy is based on counter punching. The prosecution must prove a case beyond reasonable doubt and the defence just has to find the weak links in the argument. But that proven strategy can collapse when defendants head for the witness box. They are wild cards. No matter how well briefed they can lose a case with one wrong answer. A man charged with murder can lose his temper during rigorous cross-examination and juries can take more notice of reactions than actual words. Much better to leave it to the experts.

In scores of murder trials Richter has allowed maybe only two of his clients to take the walk from the criminal dock at the back of the court to the box twelve paces away. One of the two was Mick Gatto.

'He somewhat insisted,' the barrister later remarked. Gatto likes to get his own way. The risk was that as Gatto tried to explain to the jury how he shot Veniamin in that tight corridor he might also shoot himself in the foot. But at least there were no eyewitnesses to contradict his version of events. The only other person present had lost interest in proceedings fourteen months earlier.

At first, the defence team gently took Gatto through his story about how he called Veniamin at 2.01 pm on March 23, and how the little hitman arrived at the restaurant a few minutes later. According to Gatto, he was having lunch at his unofficial Carlton office, La Porcella, and intended to visit his sick cousin at the Royal Melbourne hospital in the afternoon:

Well, when he first come in I was actually shocked that he arrived so quick because it only took him like eight or ten minutes to get there. I actually yelled out to him, 'Hello stranger', or something like that. Anyway, he come and sat next to me and there was just general talk about him being in court that day. He was at the court case there in the Melbourne Magistrates' Court and he was just going through all that.

He said that despite his concerns about the erratic killer he didn't check Veniamin to see if he had a concealed weapon, no doubt believing he was safe in such a public venue. The two sat with others at a table on the higher level of the two-tiered, large restaurant.

He actually kicked my foot under the table, and he motioned with his head like that, that he wanted to have a chat. And I said, 'Do you want to have a chat?' and he said, 'Yes, I do'. I remember pushing my chair in and walking around and giving the phone to Ron (his good friend Ron Bongetti) *in case anyone rang while I was having a chat and I'm not sure whether ... I thought he led the way but I'm not 100 per cent sure. And why I say that is I thought we were going to go outside, and actually he pointed into the kitchen, and I said 'wherever you want to go', and we walked in there.*

Question: *Who suggested the corridor?*

Answer: *He walked in. I just followed him … he turned round and he was just looking at me. I said, 'What's doing, mate?' And he said, 'I'm sick of hearing this shit.' And I said, 'What do you mean?' And he said, 'I'm still hearing that you know, you think that I'm responsible for your mate.' And I said, 'Well, I have to be honest with you, mate, that's what I keep hearing, that's what people keep saying.'*

Question: *How did he respond to that?*

Answer: *Well, there was no argument. I mean, we were just talking. Veniamin said, 'I wouldn't interfere with you because you're a mate.' I said to him, 'Well, Dino Dibra and PK were your mates, you fucking killed them.' He said, 'Well, they deserved it, they were dogs', or something like that. I said, 'Look, Andrew, I think it's better if you stay out of our company. You know, I really don't believe that you can be trusted. I'd just rather you not come around near us at all.' He just said, 'I'm sorry to hear that', or 'I'm sorry to hear', something like that, you know, and I was looking at him in the eyes, and his face went all funny and he sort of stepped back and he said, 'We had to kill Graham, we had to fucking kill Graham. Fuck him and fuck you.'…I didn't see where he pulled it from, but he stepped back and he had a gun and I just lunged at him, and I grabbed his arm, grabbed his arm with my hand, and the gun went off past my head. Went past my left. Actually I thought it hit me.* (Grazing his left ear) *It was just the loudest thing I've ever heard in my life.'*

Question: *After the gun went off you thought you'd been hit. What happened then?*

Answer: *Well, I had hold of his hand with both my hands and I sort of pushed it towards him and I … with my hands I sort of … I forced … he had his hands on the trigger and I just forced his hands, squeezed his hands to force him to pull the trigger and …*

Question: *How many times did the gun go off?*

Answer: *I know how many times it's gone off because I've heard it in evidence, but at the time I didn't know.*

Question: *How fast was all this?*

Answer: *Just like a few seconds. I mean, I remember nearly falling on the ground on top of him. He sort of pulled me over off balance.*

Question: *At some point did you finally get control of the weapon?*

Answer: *I did.*

Question: *After a number of shots went off what happened?*

Answer: *Well, I'll just explain it. When I pushed the gun towards him and I was squeezing his hand he sort of pulled me off balance and I nearly fell over on top of him and the gun was going off. It was just bang, bang. And I mean I don't know where it went or whatever. I've got to be honest, I thought I was a dead duck anyway, I thought I was gone. And like I've said, I remember nearly stumbling, landing on top of him. And I just pulled the gun out of his hand because he still had it in his hand. I pulled it out of the grip of his hand and I ran out of the hallway there, out of the corridor, into the restaurant.*

Question: *From entering that corridor to when you ran out, so from the moment you went in to the time you left that corridor, how long would you estimate that incident lasted?*

Answer: *A couple of minutes, a minute, it wasn't that long, you know. I mean, it was just that brief talk and then, you know, he just … I've never seen anyone sort of just change so quick. He just went from one extreme to another. I couldn't believe it.*

Question: *When you ran out were you holding anything?*

Answer: *I had the gun in my hand.*

Question: *Which gun is that?*

Answer: *The .38.*

Question: *It was suggested by Mr Buick* (task force investigator) *in evidence he had a working hypothesis that you fired a cover-up shot; what do you say to that?*

Answer: *That's completely ridiculous.*

Question: *It was suggested by Mr Horgan* (prosecutor) *in opening that you shot Mr Veniamin a fourth time as he lay dying on the floor of the passageway. Did you shoot Andrew Veniamin while he lay dying on the floor of the passageway?*

Answer: *No, I certainly did not. I certainly did not. He always had hold of the gun.*

In Gatto's version of events he then stepped out of the corridor and spoke to the owner of the restaurant.

Question: *Do you remember having a discussion with Michael at that point?*

Answer: *I do, yes. As we met each other, he said, 'What happened?' And I said, 'He just tried to fuckin' kill me like he killed Graham.' I said, 'Am I all right?' And at that point I put the gun in my pants, and I said, 'Is my ear all right, because I think he hit me or something?' And Michael said, 'It looks a bit red.' And then we stepped back into the kitchen. Because I was so fat, I had a big stomach; the gun nearly fell out anyway. I grabbed it and I gave it to him, and I said, 'You'd better take that.' I gave him the gun and he went and wrapped it in a towel or something; I don't know what he done with it; and put it on the bench in the kitchen area. I thought I was actually shot, you know, I thought the bullet hit me ... After that happened, I walked out of the restaurant, and as I walked over to the high level, where the boys ... they were all standing up, they didn't know what was going on ... Michael Choucair walked out of the kitchen at that point and he said, 'What'll I do?' And I said,*

'You'd better ring the police and ring an ambulance.' And then I turned around and grabbed my phone off Ronnie, and I said, 'You wouldn't believe what happened. He just tried to fuckin' kill me, this bloke. He just tried to kill me like he killed … like he tried to kill Graham', or something like that. 'He just tried to kill me like he said he killed Graham', words to that effect.

He said that when the police arrived he told them: *He pulled a gun out … he pulled out a gun and he tried to shoot me and he finished second best.*

Question: *After the shooting, how did you feel?*

Answer: *Just didn't know where I was. I was in a state of shock. I mean, I couldn't believe that I was still alive, you know. It was just my life flashed before me. The whole world was just … it was all over, you know. I thought I was a dead duck.*

He explained that he had a gun in his pocket but did not have a chance to grab it when Veniamin launched his sudden attack. *I would've been a statistic if I'd done that. If I'd tried to pull it out of my pocket, he would've shot me straight in the head. I mean, I never had time, it was just that quick. I never had a chance to go for my pocket. If I hadn't have lunged at him and grabbed him, his arm, mate, I wouldn't be here today to tell the story. I'd be a statistic.'*

Fearing that he would be charged with having an unlicensed gun, Gatto gave his .25 handgun to his good friend Brian Finn saying: *'Do me a favour, get rid of that.' And I gave him the gun, and he put it in his pocket, which is a .25 that I had on me, and he just left … I used to carry it in my right pocket from time to time, the pocket of my trousers.*

The final three questions by his lawyer were designed to leave an impression on the jury and to cut through the mass of conflicting expert testimony of the events of more than a year earlier.

Mr Gatto, you've been charged with the murder of Andrew Veniamin? Answer: *That's right.*

Question: *Did you murder Andrew Veniamin?*

Answer: *Christ, no way known. What I done is stopped him from murdering me.*

Question: *How did Andrew Veniamin die?*

Answer: *He died because he just pulled a gun at me. He went ballistic. He tried to kill me and I stopped him from doing that and he got shot rather than me. Thank God he did.*

At no stage did Gatto make the mistake of trying to disguise his mistrust of Veniamin. As he was to say elsewhere: *If it was anyone else in my position, they'd get a key to the city. It's just unfortunate that it's me.*

This frankness made it all the harder for the prosecution to undermine him. There was not much left to expose. When it was the turn of prosecutor Geoff Horgan, SC, to try to bring down the old heavyweight, Gatto would stand in the box, big fists grasping the wooden rail on either side of the elevated box, pushing his silver-framed glasses back to the top of the bridge of his nose. Refusing the traditional yes-no answers, he would take any opportunity to remind the jury of the lack of forensic evidence or what he believed were the perceived weaknesses in the prosecution case. For a slugger, he was boxing clever.

Asked why he wanted to meet Veniamin in the Carlton restaurant, he said: *Just to see his demeanour. Just to get my finger on the pulse with him, just to keep my finger on the pulse with him … there were all these rumours going around that I was going to be next and there was a possibility that he was going to do it. That's the only reason.*

He said he believed Veniamin had killed four or five times before and Horgan asked: *But you're happy to have an acquaintanceship with such a man?*

Answer: *That's right ... Let me say this, Mr Horgan, I've got hundreds of friends and ... or hundreds of acquaintances. I'm very well known, and he just fitted that category. I mean, I don't like to burn bridges; I like to establish networks of people. It always comes...'*

Question: *What networks would you establish with Andrew Veniamin, this man you believed to be a killer multiple times?*

Answer: *Well, it comes in handy with the work that I do.*

Question: *Does it?*

Answer: *It might be a building-type scenario in the western suburbs and he might know someone that's there. He runs that part of town. I mean, it's always ... you know, it's always handy to sort of ... I like to know as many people as I can.*

Horgan then wanted Gatto to say he hated Veniamin because he believed the hitman had killed his best friend, 'The Munster'. He wanted to establish a motive to back the claim that Gatto lured his enemy to the restaurant, took him to the corridor where there were with no witnesses and murdered him before setting up the self-defence scenario.

Question: *After Graham Kinniburgh was murdered, you were deeply affected by that, weren't you?*

Answer: *I was.*

Question: *Because he was a man, I think you told us yesterday, you loved?* Answer: *Yes, I did, I still do.*

Question: *Did you believe that Andrew Veniamin was responsible for that?* Answer: *I did at the time.*

Question: *Did you come to believe that he'd done it?*

Answer: *Come to believe, yes, within days. I did believe that.*

Question: *Believed that he was the murderer?*

Answer: *Yes.*

Question: *Of your dear, dear friend?*

Answer: *That's exactly right.*

Question: *And because you believed it, did you have a very strong animosity towards Andrew Veniamin?*

Answer: *Yes, probably you could say that.*

Question: *You had that same animosity up until the time of his death?*

Answer: *No, I don't agree.*

Question: *What's wrong with that?*

Answer: *Well, because we had two or three meetings where he emphatically told me that it wasn't him … And on two or three or four occasions I was satisfied that it wasn't him and had an open mind about it.*

Question: *You would loathe him?*

Answer: *I wouldn't have been happy with him, no.*

Question: *Let's not beat around the bush … You would have loathed him?*

Answer: *Yes, that's right.*

Question: *So, let's just clarify the situation. As at 23 March 2004 you did loathe Andrew Veniamin or not?*

Answer: *I wasn't sure. I wasn't sure.*

Question: *What weren't you sure about, whether you loathed (him) or whether he killed Kinniburgh?*

Answer: *Well, I wasn't sure whether he killed Graham, I wasn't sure, but as far away … as far as the way I felt about him, yes, it was certainly changed, yes.*

Horgan also wanted the jury to see that the accused man was more likely to try to take justice into his own hands than leave the investigation to police, even though Gatto's own life was in danger. According to Gatto, task force detectives had asked him about the series of unsolved murders and added 'Mick, be careful, you could be next' – a statement police denied.

I said, 'I don't know anything and if I did I wouldn't tell you anyway … I'm not an informer. I'm not a police informer. I pride myself on minding my own business.

Question: *You mean you don't believe that if a brutal murder has occurred where someone has been executed, and you know something about it, and you know the person responsible who's still running around the community executing people, you wouldn't tell the police about it?*

Answer: *Well, you never get into trouble minding your own business.*

In response to a series of questions Gatto replied: *You keep twisting it and changing it … I've told you that when I lunged at him I grabbed at his arm and his hand, but, you know, it happened that quick, the gun went off in my face. I mean, you know, I wouldn't wish upon anyone what happened to me, and I mean, to try and remember for the last fourteen months, I wake up in a cold sweat every night of the week reliving exactly what took place that day. It goes through my head every night of the week. I wake up in a cold sweat thinking about it … I was squeezing his hand. I was trying to kill him. He was trying to kill me, I was trying to kill him.*

Question: *So you've trapped his hand on the gun, so that you're capable of squeezing his finger around the gun so that he kills himself?*

Answer: *That's right, that's exactly how it happened.*

Question: *You've got control of his hand which was holding the gun?* Answer: *That's right, I'm squeezing his hand, squeezing his fingers to press the trigger.*

Question: *So he will press the trigger?*

Answer: *That's right.*

Question: *And your intention was to squeeze his hand till the gun went off, causing him to shoot himself. Was that your intention?*

Answer: *Of course it was. There's no dispute about that. I'm very happy about it, to be honest.*

JUSTICE 'Fabulous Phil' Cummins shows two signs of his personality in the big criminal trials. A judge who does not wear the traditional wig and probably the only one in Australia who wears a sparkling stud in his left earlobe, he imposes himself on trials – much to the chagrin of various defence lawyers. Some judges tend to watch passively, allowing the prosecution and defence to battle in front of the bench – speaking only when asked for a legal ruling. Their turn comes when they address the jury at the completion of the evidence. But Phil Cummins is much more a participant, through pre-trial arguments, cross-examination and closing arguments. An experienced trial advocate before he moved to the bench, he reminds a watcher of a footballer turned coach who would rather still be getting a kick than making the moves from the sidelines.

When the jury is out of the room, Cummins will question lawyers on the direction they are taking, warn them when he disagrees with their tactics and occasionally rebuke them when he feels the need. Some experienced barristers think they are kept on too tight a lead in a Cummins trial.

But when the jury enters his court, the judge's manner changes. He is both charming and protective of the twelve strangers who make up the jury, and over the weeks or months that trials can run, he develops a bond with those selected to represent the community. He appears to try to build a protective bubble for the jury, repeatedly reinforcing that only they have the common sense to deal with the issues at hand. His well-practised intimacy with strangers appears to be designed to remove the intimidation of the court setting. It is as if he and the jury have stumbled upon some bizarre circus act being performed in front of them by lawyers and witnesses. He sometimes appears to be a tour guide showing visitors the interesting spots in what can often be a dull landscape.

One of the most entertaining distractions in a high-profile trial is jury watching. Lawyers, police and neutral observers gossip about the jury members – how they sit, how they react, how they look at the accused, and how they relate to each other. Like veteran track watchers studying horses before they race, they look for the tiniest sign that could help them back a winner. But juries, like horses, can't talk so it always ends as guesswork. During the long court days some jury members are obviously bored – only half listening to hours of seemingly irrelevant evidence.

Like students in a classroom, some only truly switch on at the last minute as if preparing for their final exams. In court, the final swotting is listening to the judge's summary. While the judge is supposed to sum up the law, many jury members look for messages in the judge's charge to see which way they should jump.

Like contestants on *Who Wants To Be A Millionaire?* they hope there is a message in the delivery that can guide them to the right answer. The judge stresses that he will not and cannot do their job. He will tell them the law, but they must decide the facts.

On June 8, 2005, after a trial lasting nearly seven weeks – short by modern standards – Justice Cummins finally cut to the chase. He spoke to the jury for more than two days – reviewing the evidence and explaining the law. But it was early on day one of the summary that he explained the bases of the case, pure and simple. Who pulled the gun in the corridor? If it was Veniamin he copped his right whack and it was self-defence. If it was Gatto, it was murder: *In your decision-making, ladies and* gentlemen, you must put aside sympathy and you must put aside prejudice and decide the case solely on the evidence led here in court. Put aside completely any previous publicity. You must not decide the case on prejudice or on extraneous considerations or on sympathy but solely on the evidence led here in front of you in this court, just as you have sworn or affirmed to do.

Proceed in your decision-making, ladies and gentlemen, as you would expect and wish a judge to proceed, because each of you now is a judge, fairly, calmly, analytically and solely on the evidence. Proceed as a judge, fairly, calmly, analytically and solely on the evidence. ... In this case, ladies and gentlemen, the accused Mr Gatto, gave evidence in front of you and was cross-examined. Mr Gatto could have remained silent throughout this case and not come forward and give evidence and be cross-examined, and that is because, as I will come to in a moment, an accused person has no burden to prove anything in a criminal trial. The person who has the burden to prove in a criminal trial is the prosecution because the prosecution has brought the charge. So when you are assessing the evidence of Mr Gatto, you apply the same principles as you apply to other witnesses in the case: Is the witness telling the truth or lying? And is the witness accurate and reliable or not? But with Mr Gatto, the accused, you also are entitled to take into account in his favour that he gave evidence in front of you when he had no obligation to do so.

To be convicted of murder, the accused has to kill another person. There is no dispute about that in this case. The accused Mr Gatto says he did kill Andrew Veniamin by forcing Andrew Veniamin's finger to pull the trigger, forced by Mr Gatto by squeezing Veniamin's hand and that killed Mr Veniamin. There is no dispute about element number one, ladies and gentlemen. ... The issue here is: Who had the .38? The prosecution says Mr

Gatto had the .38, he took the deceased out the back, Gatto produced the .38 and shot the deceased repeatedly with it. That is the prosecution case. The defence says the .38 was Veniamin's. Veniamin arrived at La Porcella with the .38 hidden, and when they both went out the back, Veniamin produced the .38 and was going to shoot Mr Gatto with it. So that is the issue in a nutshell, ladies and gentlemen. No-one has suggested in this case, ladies and gentlemen, that if Veniamin had the gun and Veniamin pulled the gun on Gatto, threatening to kill him, that Gatto was not entitled to act in self-defence. No-one suggested that. If Veniamin had the gun and Veniamin pulled the gun on Gatto and threatened him, you must acquit Mr Gatto of murder. So the issue is: Who had and pulled the gun?

The accused does not have to prove he acted in self-defence. The prosecution has to prove he did not act in self-defence at the time he killed the deceased and must so prove beyond reasonable doubt. That is the burden of proof, ladies and gentlemen. Despite the use of the words 'self-defence', the accused does not have to prove he acted in self-defence. The prosecution has to prove, and prove beyond reasonable doubt, that the accused did not act in self-defence.

So, what does that all come down to, ladies and gentlemen? Who had the .38? And that is what this case has been about, ladies and gentlemen. For a conviction of murder, the prosecution must prove beyond reasonable doubt that the accused Mr Gatto produced the .38 at the restaurant and shot the deceased with it. ... So, that is what it all comes down to ladies and gentlemen. Has the prosecution proved beyond reasonable doubt that Mr Gatto had the .38? If the prosecution has proved beyond reasonable doubt that Mr Gatto had the .38 you would convict Mr Gatto of murder. If the prosecution has failed to prove that beyond reasonable doubt you must acquit him of murder.

The jury returned with a verdict on June 15, 2005, after less than 24 hours. Gatto stood in the dock, plucking at a thread that had come away from his elegant grey tie in the long minutes before the jury members returned to decide his future. His wife and daughter were in the public gallery behind him. He told them repeatedly that he loved them. He spoke calmly, quietly, assuring them everything would be all right. He and his wife, a pleasant-looking and charming woman, spoke warmly. He appeared to be more concerned for them than for himself. He made an obvious effort to control his emotions, not wanting to increase their concerns. He talked to his daughter gently about domestic matters. She said despite her father's absence some things hadn't changed – her room at home was still messy. He laughed.

When his son arrived, nervous and distressed, Gatto smiled again telling him everything would work out fine, trying to remove the building tension. It was hard not to be impressed. If a measure of a man is how he deals with life-defining moments there was no myth about Gatto that day. He told them that the most important words he would ever hear would be from the jury. The foreman would say either one word or two – 'Guilty' or 'Not Guilty'. An observer said it would be two. Gatto responded, 'I hope you're right.' To his family downstairs and his friends upstairs he repeatedly gave a Roman-like salute, right clenched fist across the heart, then fingers to the lips.

The jury of six women and six men filed in. Some were smiling, others emotional. His son had his head in his hands, shaking and close to tears. His daughter's right leg bounced with nerves. His wife just looked at her husband. As the jury came in he smiled. When the foreman announced the verdict of 'not guilty' Gatto showed emotion for the first time, pushing his glasses back as his eyes welled with relief. He then turned to his family. He thanked the judge twice as he was told he was free to go. One lawyer had previously asked him how he had remained so strong during the trial. He said he feared his family would collapse if he gave way.

Outside was the usual media throng and backslappers. Gatto told them, 'Thank God for the jury system, thank God for Robert Richter, a top barrister.' His lawyers had every reason to thank their client in return. The rumoured fee for the defence team was $400,000. That night Gatto's many supporters returned to his house for a celebration with wine, beer and pizza, ending Gatto's fourteen-month prison-inspired diet. A few days later he posed for a *Herald Sun* photographer as he relaxed in Queensland. The picture did not impress some friends of the late Andrew Veniamin.

Gatto was inundated with media requests and said he was prepared to talk for a fee to be donated to the Royal Children's hospital. For years he had donated to the Good Friday Appeal – he even managed to contribute $5000 from his prison cell while in solitary confinement. He told 3AW's award-winning breakfast team and budding investigative duo, Ross Stevenson and John Burns, 'If there is a media outlet or a talkback show that is prepared to pay a six-figure sum that goes directly to the Children's Hospital I would be more than happy to give my input and have a chat – no problem'. He confirmed he had lost 30 kilograms in jail but said he doubted if people would like to follow the program. 'I have always maintained I would rather have been fat and free. I used to shadow box in my cell because as you know I was locked up for 23 hours a day. They were calling me Hurricane Carter in there. I did it to keep focused and my mind right, otherwise you just go off you head.

'There are plenty of people in there who lost the plot and went mad. Imagine being locked in your bathroom for 23 hours then you'll sort of understand. A lot of people didn't recognise me. Some thought I had fallen ill, but I intended to lose the weight. It was the only good that came out of it. He said that following the verdict he wanted to keep out of the headlines. 'I just want to be low key and be left alone to do my own little thing. I'm going to concentrate on the building industry ... it's been pretty good to me. I want to forget about all this other nonsense. It's really got nothing to do with me anyway.'

He said he didn't feel he needed to look over his shoulder in the future and did not feel in danger while in prison. 'No, I was never in fear. That was all trumped up. There was never a problem there. I was happy to go out in the mainstream handcuffed. I said "Send me out in the mainstream handcuffed". I didn't want to be a hero but I just knew that all this nonsense was blown out of proportion. I've got no enemies. I've done nothing wrong. The bloke tried to kill me. What am I supposed to do, let him kill me? So at the end of the day I can walk around with my head held high. I'm not worried about anyone.'

Life is returning to normal for Mick Gatto. Two months after his acquittal he chanced to meet one of the authors in Lygon Street. He looked at peace with the world. He smiled and pulled back his jacket to show his stomach and he said he'd put on ten kilograms.

> He told me wherever I
> go he will find me.

2.
THE MAP MAKER

WE affectionately call them crazy, the type who can cheerfully overcome almost any hurdle to complete self-imposed challenges. The sort who climb unpronounceable mountains, run across deserts or swim tidal bays for no good reason other than to achieve the seemingly impossible. We admire their doggedness, their refusal to admit defeat and their determination to win – no matter the odds.

The record books are full of them. Crossing the Atlantic in a rowing boat, walking around Australia, sailing across Bass Strait on a windsurfer. It may be slightly nutty but it will always make the evening news – leaving the presenter with a well-practised shake of the head before crossing to the zany weather guy.

But what happens when the object of that determination is

another person rather than a mountain or an ocean? What happens when that inability to accept defeat turns into a dangerous obsession? This is a story about how our system cannot cope with the truly fixated and how the law fails to protect the innocent from the compulsive.

Robin Augustus Rishworth is a superbly fit athlete with an iron will and a never-give-up disposition. In sports mad Australia he could have become a household name if he had competed in mainstream events, but his leanings were always towards the more eccentric. Like winning the 1989 US Empire State Building climb in eleven minutes and nine seconds. Or twice climbing the 1254 stairs to win the Rialto challenge. Or climbing Uluru in thirteen minutes or cycling across the Simpson Desert without a support crew. For decades Rishworth has lived to compete, whether it be mountain biking, cross-country skiing, long-distance running or street orienteering. But he is more than an obsessive athlete. He has turned into a compulsive stalker – destroying the Olympic hopes of his victim and manipulating the justice system for years.

Like Rishworth, Belinda Phillips lived to compete. Young, stunningly fit and full of energy, she was ranked the number two female cross-country skier in Australia. And most weekends she could be found competing in some form of endurance sport. But for years she has done it in the shadow of Rishworth, a man so besotted by her that he has ignored all court-ordered restraints designed to protect her.

In July 2005, Victorian County Court Judge Joe Gullaci sent Rishworth back to jail after he again ignored court instructions to leave Phillips alone. But instead of showing any understanding of why he was going to prison, the pedantic and myopic Rishworth tried to lecture the judge then demanded an apology.

No-one in the court that day felt that jailing Rishworth would

Heavyweight watcher ... big Mick Gatto lost many kilograms on a jail diet, but don't call him Jenny Craig.

The .25 pistol Mick Gatto later recalled was in his pocket when he shot Veniamin.

Boxing clever ... a relieved Gatto outside court after beating a murder charge on a TKO.

'Benji' told his parents he would die young … he was right.

Kiss of death … sawn-off hitman Veniamin kisses heavyweight Gatto in Crown Casino.

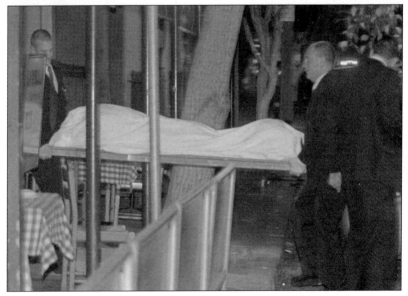

Andrew has left the building … Veniamin's body on its way to the morgue.

Pretty as a picture … Kaye in a country beauty contest before she met Graeme King.

**Unhappier days … the Kings not long before Kaye's
mysterious death.**

Family snapshot … Graeme and Kaye King with their children.

A grave mistake: Did Kaye King die 'accidently' or was she pushed?

The way we were ... the King family the way outsiders saw them.

change him but Gullaci was left with no realistic alternative. So far the court actions used to try and deal with Rishworth's stalking have involved thirteen judges and magistrates, eighteen defence solicitors and barristers and fourteen prosecutors. It has tied up police who have had to investigate his bizarre behaviour (including following him on pushbikes during a half-marathon race to observe his stalking tactics) and then give evidence in protracted court hearings.

All because Rishworth is incapable of taking no for an answer.

RISHWORTH was born prematurely in 1965 in Melbourne's east and had a conservative Catholic school education, where he was solid rather than brilliant. He competed in little athletics, played and umpired junior football but found his real passions were long-distance and solitary endurance events. He began competing in fun runs from the age of thirteen and progressed to national and world events. He had school friends but had difficulty socialising after hours, blaming his father who refused to have a phone connected to the house. He told psychiatrists that he had few girlfriends and the only sexual experience he related was when a previous girlfriend 'virtually raped me'.

He went to the Box Hill TAFE and RMIT and completed an associate diploma in mapping over six years of full and part-time study. He worked as a government surveyor for more than ten years before he was offered targeted redundancy, later starting his own mapping firm – a job that seemed perfectly suited to his personality and lifestyle.

He would travel about 60,000 kilometres a year for work and sport, eventually mapping 40 per cent of Victoria. A psychiatrist would later observe he showed 'excessive and almost compulsive behaviour at times especially around his creation of maps and his involvement in sport'.

In short, he was a loner with no love life, an obsessive nature, a determined personality, and a remarkable eye for detail. There were isolated areas of Victoria where he knew every track, every gully and every hill – which meant if someone wanted to lose themselves in Victoria's bush it was a fair bet the map maker could eventually find them. For Belinda Phillips it was just another race when she went with her sister Rebecca to Mount Buller for the Wild Man cross-country ski competition in late August 1994. Before the race she mingled with competitors as they checked their gear, stretched muscles and prepared for the gruelling event. It may be a competitive sport but many skiers remain close friends, training and socialising together.

It was here that she met and chatted briefly for the first time with the wiry and fit Robin Rishworth. They had a general conversation and she mentioned she was racing with her sister. 'We eventually raced and did not see Rishworth again,' she later said. More than two months later, on November 12, the Phillips family competed in a mountain bike race in Gembrook. The Phillips sisters won the female event and while they were waiting for the presentation Rishworth, who was not competing, came over for another seemingly harmless chat. It was clear they shared a passion for outdoor competitions and he told them about a series of suburban orienteering events that were held on mid-week evenings. Helpfully, he offered them a lift to the next week's event in Boronia.

After the race the sisters invited him to their parents' home near Woori Yallock that weekend for a family mountain bike ride. 'Once again Robin was friendly,' Belinda Phillips would tell police four years later. Rishworth was at first welcomed into Phillips' social and family circles. She found him 'friendly, outgoing, into sport and enthusiastic'. He became so comfortable he would often drop in uninvited, stay for a meal or even sleep overnight. No-one commented on why Rishworth seemed to pass by so often when he lived in Buxton, more than one hour's drive away. While he was not part of the family, he seemed happy to be at least part of the furniture.

Rishworth and Phillips, who was six years younger, competed in some team events; went out to dinner once and went on a ten-day camping trip over Easter 1995. It was then that Rishworth made a clumsy attempt to court his athletic partner while bushwalking in Gippsland.

'Robin told me he wanted to have a relationship with me and he wanted to hold my hand. He made his intentions clear, but I told him I was not interested in a physical relationship with him and I was not really interested in anyone in that way. Robin didn't really say anything after that and I thought that was the end of the subject.

'Later on in the trip, one morning, Robin tried to put his arm around me in the tent and I pushed him away and told him that I was not interested in that.'

If he felt rebuffed he didn't show it and continued to be a frequent visitor at the Phillips' home. He was even invited to the family Christmas dinner in 1995, 'because we felt sorry for him as his family did not celebrate Christmas'. But by January 1996, 'I began to get sick of Robin just turning up at my house at weekends and inviting himself to stay the whole weekend. So I told him that I needed more space and did not really want to see him every weekend, as I needed to see my other friends. Once again Robin was very amicable about what I had told him. It was also at this time that by choice I eased out of partnering Robin in events.'

But Robin Rishworth, stair climber, desert rider and fitness freak, had no intention of being eased out. He had based his life philosophy and athletic successes on pushing against the odds and trying harder when things became difficult. This, to him, was just another challenge to overcome.

NO-ONE one can pinpoint when Rishworth moved from persistent to annoying and finally to sinister. To begin with he ignored Belinda Phillips' clear messages that she wanted a life without him. At first she tried to be pleasant while distancing herself from the intense athlete, but the more she pulled back the further he intruded into her life. They had shared interests but at every race, snow event or social gathering she attended he seemed to be there – waiting, watching and looking for an opportunity to join her group. During the winter of 1996 at the Australian Cross-country Skiing Championships, at Perisher, in NSW, she met another man who shared her passion for the snow and outdoors, David Hunt. They would become boyfriend and girlfriend and would later plan to marry. But still Rishworth would not take the hint.

'I started to limit my contact with Robin at this time because he was being painful and I didn't have much time to myself. In late September 1996, I told Robin that I'd had enough of him and that I really didn't want to see him. He still came around to our house even though he was not welcome by me. My parents were also beginning to tire of his constant visits and the fact that he would invite himself for the night. It also became apparent that he was parking his car down the road from our house at night, sleeping in it and returning to our house in the mornings.'

Robin Rishworth is an accomplished cartographer and his maps of remote areas of Victoria are considered among the best ever made. He would often wander through areas of country-side to update those maps. But when members of the Phillips family saw him walking or cycling near their home, their unease increased because he lived hours away. 'Everyone in my family started to become a bit weary of Robin at this point because his behaviour seemed odd and sneaky,' Belinda Phillips wrote in a police statement.

In late 1996, she finally confronted him about being near their house at strange hours and that he had been seen near the plant nursery where she worked. 'I asked him if he was following me. He admitted that he was and he said he just had to see me. I asked him how long he had been doing this for and he said that he had it all written down and that he had been doing that for a while. This made me feel very intimidated.' She could no longer believe that he was an immature lovesick suitor. He was a determined stalker and she was the victim. Yet for some reason she chose not to go to the police but to continue to try to reason with a man who was beyond reason. Whatever tenuous grip Robin Rishworth had on reality was fast slipping away.

Phillips tried talking to him, ignoring him and avoiding him. Nothing worked. The open and uncomplicated athlete started to become closed – altering her routines and keeping secrets, even from her friends. She started to ask herself if her behaviour had somehow encouraged this strange man. Worst of all, she started to look over her shoulder as if she was the criminal. On January 5, 1997, she went on the demanding Bogong to Hotham run and four hours into the event at the remote Big River, Rishworth was waiting. 'He joined me against my wishes and ran the rest of the race, approximately two hours, next to me. I could not believe that Robin was running at my pace – he holds the national records for mountain running. Every time I stopped and walked, Robin would stop and walk.' Later he waited for hours outside a fast food store in the hope of catching a glimpse of her. 'I was beginning to feel like there was going to be no stopping Robin.' It would be part of the pattern – joining races after the start then maintaining visual contact with his target. Apparently while he loved the competition he wasn't too keen on paying the entrance fees.

She agreed to meet him in Healesville to try to persuade him to leave her alone. She could hardly tell him they were finished, as they had never started. They had not as much as held hands let alone had a significant relationship. But it would later be revealed that Rishworth had convinced himself they had effectively been a couple for two years before they had broken up. In his fantasy world they were boyfriend and girlfriend and she betrayed him by seeing David Hunt 'on the side'.

In their two-hour meeting he said he wanted her to be his girlfriend and she quickly said there was no chance. He responded by declaring he was suicidal. But for such a perfectionist he made a remarkably poor effort at taking his own life. First, he claimed he had overdosed on aspirin – but that just gave him a headache. Then he tried to gas himself in his car 'but that just made him cough for a week'. But Rishworth had reportedly tried to commit suicide years earlier and was admitted to the Larundel Psychiatric Hospital. It was claimed he dislocated his shoulder in a failed attempt to hang himself but he said the attempt was made when he was still under the effects of anaesthetic after an operation for a sporting injury.

During the meeting he told Phillips he loved her and then offered her money to advance her skiing career. Even though she was repulsed she tried to let him down gently, saying she was happy to speak to him socially if he would just stop stalking her. But the more she learned about her unwanted admirer, the more she realised he was not the type to compromise. She went to a movie and ran into a couple who had known Rishworth for years. They told her she should not be surprised at his behaviour as he was an obsessive compulsive who had followed a previous girlfriend. They told her that after the break-up the girlfriend said he would never find a girl who suited his personality. The map maker simply decided to construct the perfect girlfriend. 'They had to be non-smokers, non-drinkers and fit enough to keep up with him,' Belinda said. Love, it seems, would come later.

He listed all the women he knew who reached his standards. Some had a line drawn through them because they already had boyfriends. There were two names left. Rebecca and Belinda Phillips. 'My sister was too young so I was the only one left.' He thought there was method in his madness. He was only half right. When she started to make evening visits to David Hunt's Croydon home, Rishworth began to tell people what time she left. 'My Mum didn't even know how late I was getting home.' When a group of friends shared a house in the country town of Bright, Rishworth turned up there.

Rishworth loved the outdoors but skiing was not his main interest. Yet he started to spend more time in the snowfields – apparently to be near Belinda. When she and her family went to Lake Mountain for a run, Rishworth arrived with a cheery 'I thought you'd be here'. Belinda Phillips was an easy target – patient, non-violent and predictable. As her main interests involved competitive outdoor athletics, Rishworth could easily anticipate the events she would attend to make sure he was there. Some people manipulated by the cunning obsessive would also tip him off to her movements. She started to go to new events – enjoying the freedom or relative anonymity – but once he saw her name in the top finishers he would be there next time. Slowly the woman who loved space and freedom was finding her world shrinking.

There would be another meeting, another stalking and another confrontation – this time after a Boronia street orienteering meeting. 'I told him that he was being stupid and that he should forget me. But he just kept going on with the same stories about how he can't live without me. This was really annoying on this occasion as he was really whining and trying to gain sympathy from me. I was not interested.' But still no-one went to the police.

There was no doubt Rishworth was sinking further into his obsession and was driving thousands of kilometres following her, often able to anticipate her movements so he'd be waiting when she arrived. The meticulous map maker kept notes of her movements, later claiming he had seen her 252 times in 1995-96 before their relationship soured.

On March 21, 1997, a small group including the Phillips sisters and David Hunt left for a long weekend holiday at Lake Tali Karng – driving for four hours, hiking for half a day and crossing the Wellington River sixteen times before finally pitching their tents. The peaceful location relaxed them and the ever-present shadow of the stalker could be forgotten – at least for a few days. They chatted with a scout group camping nearby and embraced the tranquillity of the alpine 'Hidden Lake'. It was late afternoon on the last day before they packed the car and were ready to head for Melbourne. But by the time they travelled through the first town – Licola – the mood was shattered. There, parked next to the public phone box, was Rishworth's car. 'We didn't stop,' Phillips said. At the next street orienteering meeting, she asked him how he had spent his weekend.

According to Belinda, he said he had driven to the homes of her friends to confirm their cars were gone and claimed that as he had heard them talking of camping at the lake he decided to drive across the state to find them. She stood silently as he explained that he had to drive for four hours and hike for three to catch them. He set up his tent at 2am out of sight but close enough to walk into their campsite when they were asleep. She hoped it was an elaborate bluff until he told her who got up first and detailed their individual movements the next morning. He mentioned that at least he had company when he hiked out the next day – the Scout group.

She was no longer annoyed, just plain scared and felt there was now 'no real escape for me'. She asked why he had gone to the lake and his childlike response was that he had the right to go anywhere he wanted and no-one could stop him. He said just because he wasn't invited that wouldn't stop him. He then produced pages of handwritten notes with details of her movements for the previous months. She grabbed them, ripped them in half and later burned them. And still no police.

On April 24, she went with friends to a ski training camp at Mt Hotham. They left on Friday night after work and were driving through the thick fog when they passed Rishworth riding his mountain bike up the steep road. It was 1am. When a group of friends organised a dinner in Wheelers Hill, Rishworth turned up uninvited, saying he could eat wherever he wanted. Nearly every event she attended he would be there. She threw her hat off during one race and he collected it as though he was part of her support crew.

Bad weather caused the cancellation of an event at Mount Stirling so she and friends drove three hours to Lake Mountain. Again Rishworth was there. 'I have no doubt that Robin ended up following us from Stirling to Lake Mountain. It was like this situation was a detailed game for Robin.' On another occasion she went to Lake Mountain early to set up a course. He was there. She had a meeting for ski club officials. Rishworth turned up claiming he was a club representative when he was not even a member. He approached her again and she said she was going to leave the state and start a new life. 'He said he had already thought of that and it wouldn't take long to find me.'

On October 7, 1997, she was heading to work at 8.45am and was about four kilometres from home when she saw Rishworth waving a laminated sign that read 'BELINDA, YOU MADE A PROMISE'. She did not stop. But neither did he. He didn't touch her, didn't damage her property and did not threaten her. But it was Chinese water torture and he was the drip. Eventually the quietly-spoken woman reacted. 'For the first time in my life I told someone to piss off.'

On January 10, 1998, she went to Lake Jindabyne in NSW for a two-week training camp and she saw Rishworth in his car. At the end of the camp, she drove to Bright to spend the Australia Day weekend with her family. He was there. The family went out to dinner. He was there getting the table next to them. Even though the restaurant was half empty and he was dining on his own, he chose a table for four so he could be next to the Phillips' table. He began turning up at Westerfolds Park when she started early morning training with friends, choosing to park near her car.

On one trip back from Mount Buffalo with a friend she dawdled for 45 minutes after Rishworth left to make sure he was long gone. After they finally left, they stopped twice as added insurance. But two hours later he doubled back and was behind following for about 80 kilometres. They stopped to let him past – then once in front he slowed down. They ended up leap-frogging each other for most of the trip home. Another trip ruined. On April 4, 1998, she went for a run on Lake Mountain with her boyfriend. They saw Rishworth several times and when they left he again pulled out in front of them. 'I started crying and really lost control of my emotions. Robin's behaviour had finally got to the point where the quality of my life was being affected greatly.'

Finally, after more than two years of trying to deal with the obsessive, compulsive and twisted Rishworth, she went to the police. 'I thought I could handle it myself at first. Then I told a friend, an ex-policeman, and I asked him if I should go to the police and he said, "Yes, definitely".' She made a statement that said in part, 'It scares me greatly that Robin may one day snap and do something horrible to me. I often train in remote locations and by myself and feel exposed to Robin. My friends have warned me about Robin and his tantrums, I am scared he may turn on me.'

On September 21, 1998, she was granted a civil intervention order at the Ringwood Magistrates' Court. Rishworth was to have no direct contact with her. Finally she thought the police and the courts could protect her. She was wrong. Seven years later, thousands of dollars poorer, her Olympic dreams in tatters and her quality of life ruined, Belinda Phillips had moved from Melbourne to the mountains to escape Rishworth. But she was no closer to justice.

THE serial stalker became a serial litigant, returning to court again and again to try to have the terms of the intervention order varied and to fight various stalking charges. In September 1999, he was convicted in the Ringwood Magistrate's Court of stalking and sentenced to six months, wholly suspended. In February 2000, he appealed to the County Court and while the conviction stood, the suspended sentence was halved. In one hearing Belinda Phillips had to attend to give evidence and bizarrely ended up sharing a lift to the ground floor with Rishworth and his lawyer. Rishworth turned to her and said,

'We'd be a lot closer than this in ski races and presentations.' It was enough for even his barrister to tell him to shut up. The court actions continued as did the stalking. In reality he used the court process to maintain contact with his victim, forcing her to see him and relive the past.

Despite the intervention order Rishworth was given permission to continue to compete in events and pursue his commercial map making. This meant they would inevitably cross paths, but it soon became obvious Rishworth was using his racing and map making as a cover for his stalking. Phillips said that during races her stalker would try to run or ski close to her – despite being a faster runner and slower skier. In one half-marathon race, he ran 100 metres in front of her and 'constantly looked back over his shoulder at me'. She could not race at her own pace, being forced to speed to escape. For a nationally rated athlete it was a disaster.

In June 2000, she went skiing with her fiancé David Hunt at Lake Mountain. Rishworth was there – which on the surface was not surprising as he loved skiing. But despite more than 35 kilometres of trails Rishworth managed to cross their paths six times in fifteen minutes. The expert map maker knew the area well and could identify every trail crossing. 'Rishworth came down the trail from which we had just come and skied past with a grin on his face like he was playing a game of hide and seek,' Belinda said. She packed up and went home.

She quit her job and moved to Falls Creek to put distance between them but it was soon back to court as he tried to change the court order so he could map the area near her new home. He completed a new commercially-produced map of Falls Creek, popular with tourists and skiers. It shows Rishworth energetically skiing the slopes enjoying a perfect winter's day. The caption says 'East of Falls Creek' – well east it turns out. Police say the digitally altered picture was taken in Perisher, NSW. Behind him and slightly obscured is a female skier pursuing him. It is Belinda Phillips. The female figure is wearing a one-off ski suit made by Belinda for competitions. She says she will never wear it again. When she enters many of the shops at Falls Creek and Mount Beauty, the map is on display. 'It is like he is leering at me from all the shelves.'

Phillips gave up mountain bike racing and orienteering to avoid contact with Rishworth and concentrated on cross-country skiing, but in 2000 she found she could not ski without harassment. In one race he skied so close behind her he overshot a turn and she was able to ski away. 'It was as if Rishworth's main aim in that race was to ski as close to me as possible.' In August and September 2001, he was seen virtually on a daily basis at Falls Creek although he lived in Buxton. According to police, 'He frequents shelters and locations in Falls Creek where he knows Phillips will be. He places his maps in the Windy Corner shelter, where he knows she will see them. He arrives, as if by chance, at other locations where she is and follows her around ski trails.'

When she went to Perisher, he was there. When she returned to Falls Creek the following day, he was again spotted. In a summer triathlon he ran in front of her then dropped back and later waited for her to finish. At a presentation he sat two metres from her. At such events he would talk loudly so that she would know he was close. She would move, trying to place bodies between them so he could not continue to stare at her. A typical incident was documented in a prosecution report: 'The defendant lies in wait for Phillips at the Windy Corner shelter prior to the Birkenbiener Classic. He follows her out of the shelter and lays in wait for her on the trails. He videotapes her twice in two different locations. He loiters near her equipment.'

Police were able to document more than 50 alleged incidents of harassment. Even while his case was being argued in the County Court in Wangaratta, he was seen skiing at Falls Creek.

Rishworth began a series of court actions, trying to alter the intervention order and appealing judgements. In each case Phillips had to drive more than four hours to Melbourne and take time off work. 'What about the victims who want to get on with their lives and put this behind them? We are being dragged back into the courts for trivial things that are only done to harass. How long do I have to put up with this vexatious litigant wasting time and money and causing unnecessary distress? I feel like Rishworth is laughing at me, saying with all I have tried I will not get rid of him.'

He would approach people near her before races to talk to them, attend presentations when he was not a competitor, ski on the same slopes as her. When he entered a championship at Lake Mountain he wrote to the organisers perversely asking that Phillips be banned so they could not come into contact. The committee told him that she was welcome and he should not attend. Naturally he turned up for the two-day event. The woman who loved the isolation of cross-country skiing started to withdraw from the sport, although she still enjoyed coaching young skiers. But when she took some primary school children for ski lessons at Falls Creek he was there – three weeks in a row.

WHAT makes a stalker? Why do people embark on a pattern of behaviour that can only be counter-productive and self-destructive? According to Australian expert, Professor Paul Mullen, stalkers can have different personality traits but those who are organised, obsessive and determined tend to be the most difficult to sway. People such as ultra-athletes. He says there are two types of stalkers. Those who have had or feel they have had a special bond with someone and feel that when the relationship breaks up it will never be replaced. And those who feel they have been wronged and seek revenge. Some, he says, start in the first category and when they are constantly rebuffed, move to the second. 'Many have a capacity for self-deception and can convince themselves their behaviour is normal.'

Mullen says between 80 and 90 per cent of stalkers are male, mostly aged from their late teens to mid 30s, and about 80 per cent of victims are females. Figures show that five per cent of people are stalked every year and two to three per cent are stalked for weeks or months. Most cases are never reported to police. Between ten and twenty per cent of stalkers become violent. Professor Mullen says many stalkers are lonely and without friends. 'They don't tend to have people around them who in the early days can tell them their behaviour is not worth it and they should stop. It is difficult to feel sympathy for them but they lay waste to their own lives as well as their victims.'

A 2002 study on stalkers in Victoria concluded: 'The experience of being stalked is common and appears to be increasing. Ten per cent of people have been subjected at some time to an episode of protracted harassment. Assaults by stalkers are disturbingly frequent. Most victims report significant disruption to their daily functioning irrespective of exposure to associated violence.' The survey found that almost one in four respondents said they had been stalked and one in five of the victims had been physically attacked.

Professor Mullen said that while the legal system was supposed to protect stalking victims, many offenders used the courts to 'stalk by proxy'. Offenders can take frivolous civil court action forcing authorities to contact victims who are trying to move on with their lives. One man falsely told police he had been involved in a hit-run accident and had identified the registration of the second vehicle. Police found the vehicle and its owner for the alleged victim. It was a woman who had moved to the country, changed her name and altered her appearance to avoid the man. He had stalked her for six years.

Mullen said victims could be 're-victimised by the legal system'. An example he used was the case of US singer Madonna, who was stalked and threatened in the mid-1990s. When the stalker was arrested, Madonna at first refused to give evidence and when she ignored a subpoena a warrant was issued for her arrest.

Forced to testify she said, 'I feel incredibly disturbed that the man who has repeatedly threatened to take my life is sitting across from me and we have somehow made his fantasies come true. I am sitting in front of him and that is what he wants.'

Professor Mullen has found that stalkers can enjoy the court process because it maintains a relationship with their victims. Then, if the courts can fail, an obvious human response by a victim or someone close to them is to attempt to physically intimidate or attack the stalker to deter future episodes. To swat the stalker like an annoying fly. But according to Professor Mullen attacking stalkers is 'an extremely bad idea' because it legitimises violence and can result in the stalker attacking the victim.

SOME who have dealt with Rishworth say he is intelligent, extremely well organised, rigid and apparently incapable of seeing that his behaviour is morally outrageous, self-destructive and extremely stupid. His obsession has resulted in him being banned from some of the mountains that he loves, being jailed, stopped from competing in some of his favourite long-distance events and incurring massive financial burdens from his long-running court actions.

Psychiatrists are adept at dressing the most peculiar human conditions in a cloak of academic respectability. They are trained to appear non-judgmental but even the experts found little in Rishworth that was redeeming. The 1999 psychiatric report by Doctor Timothy Entwisle on Rishworth showed him to be obsessed, delusional and self-centred. '(The) examination revealed an intense, preoccupied, compulsive man – irritable, querulous and insisting upon having his say, at the same time stating that he was not being heard. He left the interview in a considerably agitated state ... It is likely he will now see me also as part of the conspiracy acting against him.' He said Rishworth was fixated with Phillips and while he had managed to rationalise his bizarre behaviour, 'It is clear that he was following her. He impressed as a somewhat emotionally cold, angry man.'

The psychiatrist said Rishworth's obsession with Phillips and his belief that he was the victim of some major conspiracy was 'of a psychotic proportion'.

Rishworth told Doctor Entwisle he sold his Buxton home of nine years to his mother before the first court case. 'I was very, very close to her. I am her closest companion. We live and share the bedroom with each other.' He told Entwisle he monitored Phillips because: 'My sole purpose was to understand what went wrong. To gather information so that I don't make the same mistake again. I am still at a complete loss to understand what's going on. She at no stage had anything to fear and it was purely an attempt by me (later on) to document what was going on.

'I parted with a great deal of money and all she ever attempted to do was to try and pull the wool over my eyes.' He said he knew there were people 'conspiring against me in this … They are also attempting to push me out of my sporting interests.' Rishworth told Entwisle his social life was poor. 'I've lost it, it's all gone. They've taken me from it.'

Four years later, nothing had changed. In 2003, Doctor Nicholas Owens found, 'Mr Rishworth believes that the victim is hell-bent on finishing off his life. He has indicated that there continued to exist a competitive rivalry between himself and the victim. His stalking behaviour will probably continue until such time as he learns that his behaviour is socially inappropriate and dispossess himself of the idea that he and the victim are engaged in some sort of ongoing competition.'

He told Doctor Owens that in the beginning his mother encouraged his relationship with Belinda, suggesting he ask her out on a date. 'He asked the victim out to an orienteering event and to tea afterwards.' Strangely, in the two meetings with psychiatrists, Rishworth confirmed that he first spoke to Belinda in 1994 but both times he said they had actually met much earlier. In one version they met at an orienteering event in 1977 and in the second they 'crossed paths' in 1980. But she was born in 1972 and would have been either five or eight at the time.

In September 1999, Ringwood Magistrate Maurice Gurvich sentenced Rishworth to six months jail, suspended for two years, and ordered him to pay $20,000 to Phillips for pain and suffering. He said, 'For stalkers such as you, it's characteristic to blame everybody but yourself.' The magistrate said Phillips, then 27, was an impressive witness and had shown 'qualities of courage and honesty' while Rishworth was 'aggressive, antagonistic and spiteful'.

Rishworth had declared in evidence that Phillips and her family had infiltrated his lifestyle and taken away his friends.

He admitted in one court hearing that he had reported Phillips to Bright police after he noticed a brake and tail-light in her car were not working. He said he was motivated by altruistic concerns for her safety.

On appeal the sentence and compensation were reduced, but it was only academic. 'It made no difference because he didn't pay. I don't think he ever intended to. But I'm still paying off the tail end of my legal debts,' Belinda said six years later.

The stalking continued and on August 13, 2003, in an appeal against a magistrate's decision, Judge Joe Gullaci said Rishworth had cynically exploited a loophole in an intervention order taken out by Phillips in 1999 that allowed him to continue competing in ski races. As he remanded Rishworth in custody pending a psychiatric evaluation, he said Rishworth was a menace and a blight on Phillips's life and that the time had come for the court to protect her. The following month he sentenced Rishworth to fourteen months jail with five months suspended. He said Phillips suffered depression and had been forced to move to avoid Rishworth. He also said the victim had considered quitting the national ski team and abandoning attempts to compete in the 2006 Winter Olympics.

Judge Gullaci said Rishworth believed Phillips needed him to compete against her to perform at her best and was convinced that legal action against him was a conspiracy to stop him racing. He said psychological reports showed Rishworth was unlikely to reform, was unrepentant and had little insight into his behaviour. When the judge then imposed an intervention order banning Rishworth from going within 50 kilometres of Falls Creek or within a kilometre of Phillips for the next ten years, Rishworth apparently fainted and was taken by ambulance to St Vincent's Hospital.

In October 14, 2004, when Judge Gullaci again tightened the

intervention order, Rishworth declared 'this is a circus' and ran from the court building. Police were about to serve him with further court documents but wisely decided not to chase the long-distance athlete. Judge Gullaci said of Rishworth, 'It's a shame that he has opted to thumb his nose at the court the way he does.'

At yet another hearing – this time at the Supreme Court on January 14, 2005 – Justice Bill Gillard said Rishworth had stalked his victim since 1996 and had not learned his lesson despite court orders and a stint in jail. 'Mr Rishworth seems to think he's above the law. I'll inform him here and now that there's no person here or anywhere in Australia that is above the law.' Despite having a nine-month suspended sentence hanging over his head, Rishworth continued to re-offend.

In July 2005, Judge Gullaci again sentenced him to jail. With 153 days he had already served before his conviction he was sentenced to a further two months. He would be released before the winter's snow had thawed. At least Belinda Phillips was spared the trauma of having to attend the hearing. While Judge Gullaci went through Rishworth's sad and obsessive past the offender sat in the dock furiously taking longhand notes. When asked to stand to hear his sentence he interrupted, pointing out that last time he had heard the judge's pronouncements he had fainted. Gullaci quietly insisted he stand. Then he asked if he could continue taking notes. The judge patiently agreed. In a bizarre postscript Rishworth demanded an apology from Judge Gullaci, claiming 'You made a false accusation that I stalked her for ten years when I didn't.' The judge said there would be no apology from his court, then sent him back to jail.

Rishworth's lawyer, James Dowsley said his client had been diagnosed with the mental illness, Asperger's syndrome – a form of high-functioning autism. Asperger's sufferers can have an obsessive interest in one subject and an intense eye for detail – a condition that Rishworth has been able to direct towards his map making. They have difficulty in socially interacting, misunderstand body language and struggle to establish and maintain relationships. Dustin Hoffman showed an obviously extreme example of the condition in the movie *Rain Man*. Like the Hoffman character, Rishworth would consider himself an 'excellent driver'. Asperger's is a condition in which sufferers range from slightly eccentric high-functioning individuals to the very odd. Hans Asperger called his young patients 'Little Professors' because of their knowledge in their chosen fields.

But the trouble with citing a medical condition in court cases is that it can paint other sufferers with the same brush. Because Rishworth suffers from Asperger's syndrome does not mean that other sufferers are likely to become stalkers. Courts have consistently found that Rishworth has been responsible for his actions.

BELINDA Phillips has been through the system too many times to see the jailing of her stalker as a victory. She wasn't there for the sentencing – 'I can't do it any more.' She has lost some of her enthusiasm for cross-country skiing and has scaled back her training regime. Next year, she hopes, the spark will return. She has been engaged to David Hunt for five years now but they still haven't set a date. She says the move to Falls Creek had not deterred Rishworth – 'I suppose four and half hours is not quite enough' and she may have to move again.

'Maybe we should stop skiing and start afresh. If he isn't going to change maybe I should. I will be 33 this year and want to start a family but I wouldn't want kids while this is going on.' She believes the stalking will continue and constant court action will prolong the harassment. 'He is a master of taking any court order and taking it to the edge. If he cannot come within one kilometre of me, he will take it to one kilometre and one centimetre. He told me wherever I go, he will find me. I just hope he can find another obsession and leave me alone.' Belinda Phillips, the enthusiastic, friendly young woman who loved the outdoors, says Rishworth has changed her, and not for the better. She says she is closed, secretive and suspicious. 'I wish I was still that person back then.'

Wangaratta Detective Sergeant Kevin Coughlan has witnessed how Rishworth has manipulated the system to feed his compulsion. 'Belinda Phillips has been the victim for years and it is tragic she has not been allowed to get on with her life. He has made himself a victim because he is unable to see that his behaviour is destroying his own life. He is clogging the courts with his obsessions and for everyone's sake I hope he is able to move on.'

But even in jail Rishworth didn't know when to butt out. While serving a previous jail term he complained regularly that prisoners' passive smoke was harming him and impacting on his fitness. Sadly, many of the inmates had not read the texts that indicate violence is counterproductive when dealing with stalkers. In response to his anti-smoking campaign they simply beat him. He spent the rest of his sentence in protection.

ONE MONTH IN THE LIFE OF BELINDA PHILLIPS.*

Robin Rishworth is on bail after being charged with stalking on July 17, 2001.

August 4. Rishworth follows Phillips at Perisher Blue, NSW. He misses the start of his own race while watching her.

August 10. Phillips sees Rishworth at Perisher.

August 11. Rishworth lodges a protest against Phillips during the National Championships at Perisher. She returns to Falls Creek that night.

August 12. Phillips encounters Rishworth on the Falls Creek trails.

August 13. For the third week in a row, Phillips 'lies in wait' for Phillips as she is about to coach children at the Falls Creek Primary School.

August 15. Rishworth reports to the Marysville police. On the same day he is seen at Falls Creek.

August 17. Charges adjourned.

August 18. Rishworth attends as a spectator at the National cross-country sprints where Phillips is competing.

August 20. Rishworth skis past Phillips at Falls Creek.

August 21. Rishworth is seen 'loitering on the course during the women's event. During presentations he sits less than two metres away'.

August 24. Rishworth follows her around Falls Creek ski trails.

August 25. Rishworth parks his car where Phillips will see it.

August 26. He leaves the car between Falls Creek and Mount Beauty, where he knows she will see it.

August 27. Rishworth 'lies in wait at the Windy Corner carpark and encounters Phillips'.

August 31. She again encounters him on the Falls Creek slopes.

* From police records.

The police are no closer to
knowing who killed Seana and
Margaret Tapp than they were
the night the bodies were found.

3.
A COLD CASE

IT was the little girl's body that got Jack. He'd seen corpses
before – too many – but when he walked from the mother's
bedroom to the daughter's, he went from hardboiled to
heartache in a moment.

Years in homicide had got him used to staring down terrible
sights, masking anger and disgust with blank eyes and black
humour. But this almost seemed so peaceful, so normal, that it
got under his guard.

She was in bed, quilt pulled up by whoever had raped and
strangled her after killing her mother. You'd think she was
asleep. Her name was Seana Tapp and she was only nine years
old.

The memory of the murdered girl has stuck with Jack Jacobs
for years, while so much else about the case has faded away.

'When I saw her I cried,' he says, staring into his drink. 'She was the same age as my daughter...'

Dead kids are every copper's nightmare. The retired detective senior sergeant fiddles with his glass, sighs and changes the subject.

Facts are safer than feelings. The trouble is, he admits, with this case the facts were hard to find. Still are. Only one stands out: the police are no closer to knowing who killed Seana and Margaret Tapp than they were the night the bodies were found on August 8, 1984. Even then, the trail was already 18 hours old, and cooling fast.

There are about 280 'cold cases' on the Victorian homicide squad unsolved files, dating from the 1950s. There are another 400 in NSW, more than 1000 throughout Australia. This is just one of them, a brutal double murder of a mother and child that had no apparent motive, scant publicity and no obvious suspect ... but many potential ones.

Some people have been ruled out by forensic tests. Too many others, meanwhile, have to put up with gossip and innuendo as they wait for police to clear their names.

THE last to see the Tapps alive were their next-door neighbours, the day before. Karen Bomford, 11, usually played with Seana, but the pair had argued on that Tuesday afternoon while walking home from Wattleview Primary School near their homes in Kelvin Drive, Ferntree Gully, in Melbourne's outer east.

Later, about 4.30pm, Karen saw Seana riding her bike but did not join her. Neither did Melanie Harris, from across the street.

The three girls often played together and stayed overnight at each other's houses.

But this night none of them played with Seana, the result of a schoolgirl tiff that now, twenty years on, still troubles them because of what happened to their playmate.

About 4.45pm, a neighbour glanced at the Tapps' house and saw Margaret sitting in the lounge room, studying, as she often did.

Margaret was a divorced nurse with two children, a wide circle of friends and many ambitions. She had gone back to school in her 30s then enrolled in law at Monash University with the aim of becoming a medico-legal specialist. At 35, she was doing third year and often seen poring over her books late at night. Her 14-year-old son, Justin, had gone to live with her parents and she and Seana had settled into a routine.

One challenge was not enough for the restless Margaret. She was combining part-time work, parenting and legal studies with learning to drive a semi-trailer, taught by a young man eager to give the friendly nurse free lessons. Characteristically, she wanted the truck licence so she could help country friends harvest their crop. That was Margaret Tapp, her friends say, impulsive and generous.

At 7.30 that evening, Margaret made two quick calls. One was to 'Jim', a 44-year-old widower who often accompanied her on outings. She sometimes complained good-naturedly to other friends about Jim's attentions, but perhaps she depended on him for company more than she let on. She told him she had opera tickets for the following night, if he wanted to go. She wanted to keep the relationship platonic, but she certainly had no reason to fear him.

As usual, Jim accepted immediately. The gentle Scottish-born carpenter had admired Margaret for years. They'd been neighbours before her split with Don Tapp five years before, and she had helped nurse Jim's dying wife in 1977. Such kindness was typical, according to her friends. She had a warm heart – and she broke hearts. Her extroverted personality and good looks attracted men whether she wanted them or not.

Next, Margaret called her friends Penny and John Rumble and asked them to babysit Seana the following night. John spoke to her. Margaret was vague about her plans – saying she was going to 'have dinner with someone', rather than revealing she was going to the opera with Jim.

THE Rumbles loved Marg Tapp. She and another nursing friend turned up every week to help bathe Penny Rumble's mother, Jan Young, who had multiple sclerosis. Jan, although older, had nursed with Margaret at the William Angliss Hospital in Ferntree Gully and was probably the younger woman's closest confidante. There was plenty to confide about in Margaret's stormy private life.

It was late winter, evenings were dark and chilly and the Los Angeles Olympics were on. Most people stayed indoors to catch the Games highlights.

Rosalind Bomford didn't. Rosalind, who lived next door with her husband Jeff, was a cook at a local pub, the Royal Hotel. It was evening work, and afterwards she went playing bingo with friends at another hotel and so didn't get home until just after 10.30pm. She watched the Games with her husband. It was the night the Australian long jumper Gary Honey made the leap of his life to win the silver medal behind the great Carl Lewis. About half an hour later, she heard something strange: 'A scream – a muffled sort of thing.'

Rosalind stood up, looked out the window and joked about a notoriously rough woman who lived in the street: 'It's probably [name deleted] murdering somebody.' She asked Jeff what time it was. 'Ten past 11,' he said.

As Rosalind prepared for bed just before midnight, she was in the bathroom with the door ajar when her dog, which was inside, growled at the back door. Rosalind was sure someone was outside. She checked that the door was locked and went to bed. She didn't sleep well.

Across the street, Jack and Loreen McNamara were already asleep. But just after midnight they were woken by Seana Tapp's pet cocker spaniel, barking and howling. It was a meek little dog that they had never heard bark at night before.

AS Karen Bomford set off for school about 8.30 the next morning, she remembered the argument and decided not to drop in next door to see if Seana wanted to walk with her. The blinds were still closed at number 13. She assumed Seana and her mother were sleeping in, which was not unusual.

The blinds stayed drawn. In mid-afternoon Tony Blackwell, the young man then going out with Margaret's older sister, called around to visit.

He picked up the morning newspaper from the driveway, dropped it at the front door and knocked, then tapped on a window. Puzzled that Margaret's green Corolla was there but no-one was home, he left.

By the end of the working day, no-one in the house had stirred. At dusk, when other houses had lights on, the Tapps' place was in darkness. Just after 6pm, Jim the carpenter arrived to pick up Margaret to go to the opera. A regular visitor, he knew the Bomfords by sight. He also knew what Tony Blackwell didn't – that the sliding door at the back of Margaret's house didn't lock. Seana and the girl from over the road, Melanie Harris, had accidentally broken it while playing a few weeks before, and the easygoing Margaret had not had it fixed.

When no-one answered his knock, Jim let himself in. The

kitchen and living room were empty. He went to Margaret's bedroom. Bedclothes covered her body, but as soon as he saw her face, he knew the worst.

Jeff Bomford remembers Jim banging on his door. 'He was pale and upset and was looking for Seana,' Bomford recalls. 'He said to me: "Jeff, it's bad. It's real bad." He was hoping Seana was staying with us. He knew Marg had a few problems and he thought she had done herself in.' But Seana wasn't with the Bomfords. That's when they both knew it seemed even more sinister than suicide. Jim called the police.

Twenty years on, his voice still cracks when he tries to talk about that night.

JACK Jacobs got the call at 6.43pm. He and the then youngest member of his homicide crew, Rod Wilson, lived near each other and were driving homewards together when the police radio diverted them to Ferntree Gully. They pulled up outside 13 Kelvin Drive at 7.02, according to the meticulous notes Jacobs made.

Number 13 might have been the unluckiest house in Australia that day, but it looked ordinary enough. It was a brown, brick-veneer about 100 metres from Burwood Highway, close enough to hear the traffic hum, but otherwise a quiet residential street where most people knew each other.

Local police had the scene sealed off and a distressed man hunched in a police car. The two dead were both strangled, they told the detectives. No sign of a struggle or forced entry. A pizza box in the oven with some dried-up pieces left in it.

Jacobs looked at the dead woman in the main bedroom. He could see the strangulation marks on her throat from the doorway. There were two empty Arnotts chip packets on the bed, and a law book she had apparently been reading before it all went wrong. He walked to the rear bedroom and saw the little girl's body and it got him: a stab to the heart of a father who worked long hours away from home, methodically sifting the wreckage of other families' lives as his own trickled away.

At first, it looked like a 'domestic', the description used in the first D-24 radio call. Most homicides are – arguments between partners that flare into murderous rage, one mad act in otherwise mundane lives. Police are trained to have open minds – 'a mind is like a parachute,' goes the standard lecture, 'unless it's open it doesn't work.' But, in the field, until the evidence points elsewhere, whoever reports a death is automatically top of a short list of suspects.

Which meant that Jim, the dead woman's would-be boyfriend, would be doing some explaining before he was cleared. Meanwhile, the forensic people searched the scene – though not so thoroughly that they found Margaret's jewellery hidden underneath her mattress. A relative was surprised to find it there much later, something that made him wonder about the efficiency of the police inquiry.

In 1984, DNA testing was still wishful thinking; fingerprints were the greatest investigative tool. Several prints were found but eliminated on the grounds that they belonged to friends, neighbours or relatives who could have legitimately been at the house. Ironically, knowing the victims could mask a killer.

Not only were there no unknown prints, but the experts who combed the house for evidence found frustratingly little – and nothing to give detectives an easy lead.

There were two different types of hair on Seana's clothing and bedclothes: a long blond hair and some shorter grey ones that might have been tinted. But hairs could have come from anywhere, any time. Hair might confirm a suspect, but not identify one.

However, two other clues found at the scene could one day trap the killer. First, the semen stains on Seana's nightdress. In 1984, it was not possible to identify the killer's blood group from the sample, but after the mid-1990s it was possible to get something much better – a DNA profile unique to one person in millions. Second, there were fresh Dunlop Volley tennis shoe prints in Margaret Tapp's bedroom and in the bathroom. The shoe size proved they were not Margaret's or Seana's. Nor did they belong to anyone else that police could legitimately place at the scene. Detectives concluded that the shoe prints probably belonged to the killer. Nothing has changed that view since 1984.

A lot can happen in 20 years. People change their looks, their names, their cars and their addresses – but they can't change their DNA or their feet. Catching the killer is a case of finding the perfect match.

One day, the Tapp case will come to the top of the pile of files that the specialist 'cold case' detectives are constantly reviewing. They can only hope that the investigators of 1984 gathered enough names to let them trace everyone who might have been in contact with the Tapps.

Regardless of forensic wizardry in the laboratory, in the streets detectives still need doors to knock on. DNA testing doesn't mean much until investigators track down the right suspect and force him to face the moment of truth.

Chances are, of course, the killer has slipped under the radar. Meanwhile, every man even remotely connected to the victim deserves to be checked and eliminated from the investigation for good.

Before the homicide squad arrived at Kelvin Drive, a local detective, Ken Mahon, had questioned Jim the carpenter in the police car. Later, as others started a doorknock in the street,

Mahon took a detailed statement from Jim at the local station. Then Jacobs' crew took over.

It was a torrid few days for the carpenter as detectives tested his story from every angle. They drew the same conclusion as Mahon had: Jim was genuinely devastated and did not falter on any detail.

Jim's ordeal differed from that of his neighbour and Margaret's former husband, Don Tapp. It was cruel but necessary that Seana's stricken father be eliminated as a potential suspect. Fortunately he had a watertight alibi: he had been with his new partner and her family all Tuesday evening.

Jim's story took a little longer to verify.

By the time police were satisfied he'd had no opportunity to commit the murders – let alone the desire to do so – the trail had split a dozen ways.

It wasn't that there were no suspects. There were too many. One was a former policeman, a fact that would stay submerged for 20 years.

THE detectives probably would have found the man eventually anyway, but what made him appear more interesting was that Margaret's sister Joan volunteered his name soon after arriving at the murder scene.

After police interviewed Joan, she recalled something Margaret had confided to her a few days before.

A friend of the family's – a retired policeman who knew her father well from the Masonic Lodge – had been visiting Margaret.

He had brought flowers and lent her books on sailing, which she had tried on visits to the Gippsland lakes. But Margaret had apparently taken the older man's attentions the wrong way. Used to attracting men, she assumed he was just another unwanted admirer, albeit an especially embarrassing one, because he was a friend of her father's and much older.

Melanie, Seana's friend from across the road, also sensed something was wrong. After the murder she tried to tell her mother and others that Jim was not Margaret's boyfriend, and that other men had been around. Melanie insisted that she remembered seeing Margaret so annoyed at getting a bunch of flowers from someone that she screwed up the card that came with them.

The former policeman, then in his 50s, had resigned early from the force. Years before, as a teenager, Margaret had run away from home and it was he who had found her and brought her home to her grateful parents.

In 1984, this man owned a remote country property in eastern Victoria that Margaret and her children visited not long before her death.

He had taken the last known photograph of her and her children, sitting on a log in a hilly paddock. Margaret gave the snap to a friend, Sally Stevens, who later showed it to the author.

In some ways the ex-policeman seemed as logical a suspect as Jim the carpenter, yet he was fortunate enough to avoid any publicity.

He later told Margaret's parents he had been questioned at length about the murders, but few outside the police force knew that.

Although the man was officially written out of the story – he was not named or included in the 1986 inquest brief – he was more fortunate than other potential suspects in that any lingering doubts about him were finally lifted in the late 1990s, when he was one of just three men discreetly cleared by DNA testing, according to police. The other two men eliminated the same way were the subject of even more delicate inquiries, both as a result of 'tip-offs'.

One was a married surgeon who had supposedly had an affair with Margaret Tapp. The other was a man who had received a large loan from the widow of another of Margaret Tapp's lovers. No thriller writer would dare invent a plot with so many twists.

The strange thing about the Tapp murders is that they got such little publicity. The apparently random killing of a mother and child in their beds had all the elements of a suburban horror story that would ignite public outrage. It never did. It should have made headlines and news bulletins for days – and again when the inquest eventually reached the coroner's court in 1986. But without the usual trickle of information from police sources, official and otherwise, the story died fast and barely registered with the public.

A couple of mundane stories and a few tiny 'briefs' appeared in Melbourne's then three daily newspapers and, without fresh angles, television and radio coverage soon dried up. It meant that only friends, family and neighbours of the victims were to remember it. Even the police directly involved say they remember other cases more clearly.

One reason for the lack of publicity was that the police found no new leads – or at least nothing they were willing to broadcast to attract information from the public. By contrast, the murder six months earlier of a woman called Nanette Ellis in the neighbouring suburb of Boronia won plenty of media coverage and concentrated police attention.

Interestingly, Jack Jacobs' overworked crew also handled the Ellis inquiry, which was to stick in Jacobs' mind far more than the Tapp mystery.

There were other reasons for the low-key coverage. Margaret

Tapp's family was publicity-shy and quietly discouraged her friends from talking to the media.

They were a respected local family who had lived in the area since the 1950s, when it had begun to change from small farms and orchards into suburbia. Margaret's father was in the Masonic Lodge and her mother was a teacher and churchgoer. They were deeply respectable people mortified by any suggestion of family scandal.

Their reaction was understandable. Nothing could bring back their dead, so there was no point raking over things that might cause more pain – especially for Margaret's teenage son, Justin, who had been living with his grandparents at their Gippsland holiday house when his mother and sister were killed.

The problem for the family and the police was that Margaret's tangled private life complicated things. It meant there were other people, some of them with clout, who stood to be embarrassed by what might come out.

By the standards of a conservative older generation, Margaret Tapp was a modern, liberated woman. She hungered for knowledge and new experiences. She was impulsive and generous.

Her friend Sally Stevens describes 'a stunning woman' who turned heads: 'She had red hair and a peaches and cream complexion and she didn't realise the effect she had on people, which made her all the more appealing.' She attracted men and she broke hearts.

After leaving her husband five years before, Margaret had embarked on a series of affairs – at least four of them with medical specialists. The first of these was with an anaesthetist, who had a breakdown when the affair ended. Affairs with a surgeon and a urologist didn't last, either. But another, with 'Dr John', a gynaecologist and obstetrician, was more serious. He bought her the Kelvin Drive house in 1981, installed her as a 'tenant' and helped support her while she studied.

It was a stormy relationship. Dr John, to that date a sober and hard-working Lutheran with three children, was torn between his wife and family and the beautiful nurse.

He often visited Kelvin Drive but always returned to his family in the Dandenongs. Margaret told friends the dour doctor was the love of her life, and she was increasingly agitated that he wouldn't quite leave home for her. Neighbours often heard them argue and she once damaged his prized Datsun sports car.

In early 1983 Margaret went to America. The trip was meant to help her get over Dr John, who had told his wife the affair was dead. Instead, within days of Margaret's return, he was dead – killed when his sports car ran off a treacherous (but familiar) mountain road in the early hours of the morning as he raced to deliver a baby.

Road accidents happen every week – especially to tired and emotional people driving fast after midnight – but the doctor's death caused a wave of rumour and innuendo aimed at his grieving widow's supposed motives for hurting him. So when his former lover and her daughter were murdered 16 months later, the local rumour mill ran hot with far-fetched Agatha Christie plotlines peddled by armchair sleuths and idle gossips. The coincidence of the deaths was so dazzling that it misled many people into ignoring the lack of any logical connection – let alone evidence. Sound reasoning never stopped foul rumour.

The fact that the doctor's shattered widow was a practising Christian who had reached an amicable financial settlement with Margaret Tapp over the Kelvin Drive house did not deter the gossips and their bizarre theories.

The victims' relatives needed someone to blame, and anyone

would do. Playing the blame game is a basic human response to trauma, though not always a rational one. Demonising Dr John's widow, no matter how illogical that was, blinded Margaret Tapp's relatives to a more likely scenario – that the killer might have been closer to home. It also ignored the fact that several other doctors' wives had as much motive as Dr John's widow to hate the amorous Margaret.

Margaret's brother Lindsay, a former soldier who was deeply disturbed by the murders, now admits he was once obsessed with the idea that the doctor's widow might have been involved, but later realised how silly that was. Lindsay had served in the army and was a good rifle marksman and keen hunter as a young man.

Deeply disturbed by the murders, he told friends he would consider shooting anyone that he was '99 per cent' sure was implicated in his sister and niece's murder. Fortunately, he gave up revenge fantasies without doing anything. And after the Port Arthur massacre in Tasmania in 1996, he gave up his guns – handing in all 14 of them.

The irony in all this was that he himself might have sat on the strongest clue for twenty years without realising. And no-one had thought to ask him.

'WE had a lot of half-baked suspects but no good ones,' muses Jack Jacobs. He is sitting in his new, bayside apartment, red wine in hand and his old police notes in a thick folder on the table. He is middle-aged, mild-mannered, medium-sized – the nice one in the good cop, bad cop routines. A compulsive note-taker then and now, he even recorded the names and colouring of the Tapps' cats, Louie (black and white) and Moses (ginger), at the crime scene. He also noted some more useful details.

He produces faded photocopies of the Dunlop Volley tennis

shoe prints, a tantalising clue to the killer. Trouble is, he says, the brand was so common there was a pair in every other house.

Anything else? There was, he ventures, one other lead as promising now as it was in 1984.

A red Falcon utility with distinctive mag wheels was parked near the Tapps' house on the night of the killings. Two local youths saw it. One noticed it had a black tarpaulin, gold striping along the side and the fancy '12-slot' wheels.

Detectives traced dozens of red utes but not the right one. They even tried hypnosis to see if the witnesses could recall number plates or other details. But the ute investigation petered out and even the victims' family forgot it.

In 1984, Margaret's brother worked for the body responsible for supplying Melbourne's water. He was a maintenance worker, one of a gang that mended burst water mains, relaid pipes, painted hydrants and chipped weeds. They were a knockabout lot who often drank together after work at their depot.

Probably the most knockabout of all – 'a shifty, strange sort of bloke,' one recalls – was a man in his 30s who drove one of the depot tip trucks.

He was not disliked, but some workmates were wary of him. Strong and quick-tempered, he had once jumped out of his car in peak-hour traffic and smashed another driver's side window with his fist after being cut off. He was a rule-breaker who was eventually sacked for rorting overtime and for thieving. If anyone wanted a cheap truckload of loam, he would steal it from the supply yard. And if someone wanted to 'borrow' the truck for a private job, he would be in it if there was something in it for him.

So, some time in mid-1984, when Margaret's brother wanted to move a kitchen table from his house to hers, he asked the driver. They picked up the table in the truck and took it to Margaret's and carried it inside.

Margaret and Seana were killed soon afterwards. In the nightmare of the following months, Margaret's brother forgot all about the visit in the truck. He did not attach any significance to it then. Had the police talked to him, he might not have mentioned it anyway because 'borrowing' the truck might have cost him his job. It happened sometimes: the truck driver was later sacked when caught smashing fire hydrants with a crow bar so he could get penalty rates and extra time off for fixing the damage after hours.

Recently, Margaret's brother thought about the tip-truck driver for the first time in years. He recalled the story about dropping off the table in the truck. Then, asked if he had known anyone who drove a red Falcon ute with 12-slot mag wheels in 1984, he went quiet and lit another in an endless chain of cigarettes.

The truck driver had a few flashy Fords in those days, he said, dragging hard on his smoke. One of them was a maroon ute with 12-slot mags.

The former truck driver lives five minutes drive from Ferntree Gully. Unlike most others who worked with Margaret's brother at the maintenance depot, he says he never heard about the double murder. He didn't read newspapers, watch television, listen to the radio or discuss it with his workmates, he says. And he doesn't want to talk about it, thanks.

To Victoria's cold case squad, the tip-truck driver is just one more potential suspect who is entitled to be cleared, a name to be added to a growing list of men who, ideally, should all be DNA-tested.

Some people were spoken to by police in 1984, others

perhaps should have been but weren't because the overworked homicide crew had no time to eliminate every possibility. Even Margaret's brother should have been eliminated, but he can't recall even being spoken to in 1984. Neither, astonishingly, were any of his friends or workmates – although at least one has been since this story was researched in 2004.

Among those who would like to be cleared in the Tapp case are the male members of a rowdy family that moved away from Kelvin Drive soon after the murders, much to the neighbours' relief. One of them, then 23, finished late shift at a nearby factory at 11.30pm that Tuesday – exactly the right time to be 'in the frame', as he himself willingly admits. He also volunteers that his older brother (and a brother-in-law, a violent sex offender later jailed for rape) were not properly eliminated. Then there was his teenage brother – call him 'Benny' –a youth distrusted by every woman in the street except the easygoing and kindhearted Margaret Tapp.

Glenda Harris, then a single mother, lived opposite the Tapps. She vividly recalls Benny, then 15, blocking the footpath and making suggestive comments to her and her young daughter. 'He had a filthy body and a filthy mind,' she says. 'I warned Margaret against letting him in the house near Seana, but she let him hang around.'

While others avoided Benny, he repaid Margaret's kindness by mowing her lawns and servicing her Corolla car. But even she was annoyed about the way he would turn up unannounced and come in the unlocked back door.

Benny still likes talking about Margaret. He went to her funeral, visits her grave, and happily (and accurately) directs a stranger to her 'speckly brown' headstone with its gold letter-ing, just near the boundary fence of the Ferntree Gully cemetery.

One Sunday in August this year, just after the 20th anniversary of the murders, Benny drove down his old street, pulled up opposite number 13 and had a chat to the neighbours. They talked about the murder.

Since then, Benny has said he wants to know if the detectives are going to come back and find out what happened to the woman who was kind to him.

'Margaret was my friend,' he told the authors. 'She had a heart of gold.'

She had two black eyes and a broken nose. She said she had walked into a door ...

4.
GETTING AWAY WITH MURDER

NO-ONE can say for sure how long it takes to squeeze the very life from another human. If the victim is lucky, the throat can be grabbed in such a way that minor pressure stops the heart and death is virtually instantaneous. But Julie Ramage, 42, was not one of the lucky ones. As she lay on the floor of the partially renovated family room with her husband's hands around her neck, she could not scream because her vocal cords were already constricted. But that didn't matter because there was no-one who cared close enough to hear. Her husband had made sure of that.

Struck twice with punches delivered with such force that his right hand was swollen and red a day later, she was already bleeding from small cuts to the left side of her nose and mouth when she fell to the ground. The big bruise just over her left ear may have been caused by the fall and pathologist Dr Matthew

Lynch would later say 'this may have resulted in a degree of incapacitation'. But bruises and cuts on both her hands indicated that Julie Ramage did fight for her life against the man she had once loved, but had long ago learned to fear.

According to pathologist and Associate Professor David Ranson, the pressure applied in such strangulation cases can vary but must be constant and sustained. Imagine trying to open a stubborn jar or squeezing the juice from a ripe orange by hand. Or grabbing an arm so hard it leaves an angry bruise for days. The pressure must be maintained for between 40 seconds and a few minutes depending on how long the victim can maintain a struggle. Then as the air and blood flow is stopped, the capillaries in the eyelids burst and the victim loses consciousness. People can kill in a split second – an unlucky punch, the squeeze of a trigger or an artery nicked by a sharp-edged weapon. But slow strangulation requires both strength and determination. And James Ramage, schoolboy rugby player turned aggressive self-made man, had plenty of both.

In his rambling 'confession' delivered to Senior Detective Darren Wiseman of the homicide squad 24 hours after he killed, he claimed he was not really sure how long his wife struggled. 'Look, I … I had just lost the plot. I remember hitting her once or twice and then just strangling her … I just remember holding her neck.'

Wiseman asked, 'Was she fighting?'

Ramage replied, 'She did for a bit, but not for long.'

Despite his confession that he had attacked his wife without warning, that she was unarmed and unable to defend herself – just over a year later a jury would accept that he had acted under provocation so great that his crime was reduced from murder to manslaughter. So while no-one doubts that James Stuart Ramage is a killer, in the eyes of the law he is no murderer.

The story of how Jamie Ramage took a life and ruined his own in just a few minutes began three decades earlier and half a world away when he met an attractive and outgoing teenage girl and they decided to marry too young and too soon.

ENGLISH-BORN Julie Anne Garrett and her twin sister Jane were the sort of kids who were never short of company and always looked destined to succeed. Pretty, bright and sporty they had a large circle of friends while growing up in the township of Cheshunt, not far from London. While parents Patricia and Ray were building businesses, first with a corner shop and finally with two supermarkets, the twins became heavily involved in sport including tennis, netball and sailing. Julie represented her county in athletics and began a life-long love affair with horse riding.

James Ramage – Jamie to his friends – was born in Melbourne on April 9, 1959, to Joyce and James. The family, including his two younger brothers, moved to Hertfordshire where Jamie went to Cheshunt Secondary School completing his A-levels and excelling at contact sports such as rugby.

Julie had a few boyfriends by the time she met the well-travelled eighteen-year-old, who was then going out with one of her best friends. Soon Julie and Jamie became inseparable. According to Patricia the seventeen-year-old Julie was taken with Jamie. 'She thought he was flash – he had the use of an impressive car. She was pretty impressed.' Twin sister Jane was less so. 'My first impression of Jamie was that he was very self-assured. He was always boasting about his sporting prowess. He was a snob.' The twins' father remembers his first impressions of the assured teenage boy with ambitions and an attitude. 'He seemed like a young man who knew where he was going,' he said with typical understatement.

But he had a small insight into the character of the man who would one day be his son-in-law, during an inconsequential spat in the house between Julie and her new boyfriend. 'Jamie charged upstairs like a madman – he started yelling at Julie. I was appalled really. I told him that if there was any need for my daughter to be chastised then it was up to me. It was after this incident that I realised that Jamie could be a hothead.' But at seventeen Julie had neither the experience nor the desire to search for partially hidden character flaws in her good-looking boyfriend.

Jamie had his future planned and he knew it was back in Australia. On completing secondary school his family had arranged for him to return to Melbourne, where a wealthy friend would provide an entrée to the big end of town. In September 1978, the Garretts held an eighteenth birthday party in a community hall for the twin girls. It was at that large gathering that Julie told her parents she would follow Jamie to Melbourne. 'She then showed us the engagement ring. It was a solitaire diamond ring … At the time it broke my heart,' Patricia said.

The Garretts had raised the twins to be independent, even sending them to different schools in their senior years and although they had doubts, they were prepared to support Julie's decision. But there was something else that jarred. The young Ramage had not bothered to talk to them about taking their daughter to the other side of the world. 'I found it pretty rude that Jamie had not asked for Julie's hand in marriage. In those days it was customary to do so,' Patricia Garrett said.

About three months later, Jamie left for Melbourne while Julie worked for a bank in London. The girl with the wide network of friends stopped socialising and began saving for her trip to Australia. Meanwhile Jamie was getting a quick course in business and networking through his family friend. Julie's twin Jane said the friend was 'well off and Jamie was living a privileged lifestyle. He was mixing with the social set'. But it would be wrong to suggest that success was handed to him on a plate. Jamie worked full-time during the day and studied accounting at night. He was always determined to find the fast track to success. He held business management positions in Hardie Industries, Country Road and McDonalds, before establishing his own companies.

On March 16, 1979, Julie flew to Melbourne and initially lived with her uncle, Alf Kellett, in Preston before moving in with Jamie in a small unit in Black Rock. According to Jane, Uncle Alf arrived in Australia in the 1920s aged just seven. 'He was a classic Australian working-class man.' Perhaps too classic for the ambitious and social-conscious Ramage. 'He took a dislike to Alf and his family because they were working class. Initially they socialised with Alf but over the years Jamie chose to sever the relationship with Alf and his family.' The couple flew back to England in December as part of a round-the-world-trip. 'When Julie returned she looked fabulous, she looked so happy,' Jane said.

But there was still tension. The Garrets planned a 'small, quaint wedding', but the groom wanted the celebration to be on a grand scale. Eventually it was agreed the reception would be extended at a cost of 400 pounds with the excess to be split between the two families. 'What really sticks out is when Jamie went to give us the 200 pounds, he just walked in and threw the envelope at us … I suppose looking back it was an indication as to how Jamie was going to treat people,' Patricia would recall almost 25 years later.

They were married on January 5, 1980, and then returned to Melbourne. Any lingering resentment was buried when two years later the Garretts holidayed in Australia. Julie and Jamie were perfect hosts – taking the couple to Lorne, Yarrawonga and the Gold Coast. So impressed were Patricia and Ray they decided to follow their daughter and immigrated the following year. Jane was also to move but she had met her future husband, Howard. They would settle in Melbourne later. Ray and Pat arrived in August 1983 and for six weeks they stayed with Julie and Jamie at their home in Percy Street, Balwyn. The couple found jobs, bought cars and were looking for a house within three weeks.

For independent people it can be hard to adapt to the routines of others, but even so the Garretts quickly felt they had soon outworn their welcome. According to Patricia, 'Jamie became overbearing.'

He made it clear that the house revolved around him. If he was caught up at work, then dinner was delayed until he was ready. 'Although we were all adults and working we had to wait for Jamie,' she said. If Julie found this strange she kept her thoughts to herself. Ray found that Jamie needed to feel that he was always in charge. 'If he was in a situation he couldn't control, he would grab Julie and leave ... Anyone who didn't have the same opinion as him, he didn't want to know.'

Being an inflexible control freak was one thing but soon the in-laws sensed an undercurrent of intimidating violence. Patricia recounted, 'I can also recall when Ray and I found a hole in the living room plaster. Jamie had punched a hole in the wall. I spoke to Julie about the hole ... She tended to laugh it off and said that Jamie didn't know his own strength.' There were other warning signs – a wedding gift painting that had hung on the wall disappeared. Julie told her parents that Jamie had destroyed it. At the age of eleven Julie had collected some delicate French china but now when her mother tried to give her

Rooftop's
Large Text Edition

Falls Creek
Ski Touring Map

Includes:Howmans Gap, Cope Hut - Tawonga Huts - Mt. Nelse
- Spion Kopje - Pretty Valley & Kangaroo Hoppet Race Course
Ideal for school groups and suitable for day and overnight tours

Skiing east of Falls Creek, in the Australian Alps

**A taunting image … map maker Robin Rishworth
used a picture with his victim in the background.**

Haunted … Belinda Phillips endured years of stalking before telling Rishworth to 'piss off'.

Loneliness of the long distance runner … Robin Rishworth stalks out of court.

A smile to die for? Margaret Tapp was vivacious, friendly and attracted men.

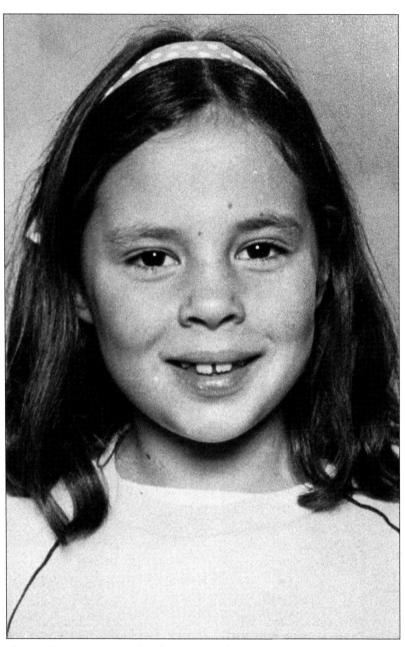

Seana Tapp … strangled in bed at nine years old.

Former abalone poacher Cam Strachan on a Bass Strait island.

**Millionaire John Seaton …
destroyed by doping accusations.**

**Robert Asquith (left) … slow
horses, fast bucks, mysterious
death.**

the collection she refused without explanation. Patricia believed she feared that Jamie would smash it during one of his rages.

In 1984 came the first of several attempts by Julie to break free. But she would always return when her domineering husband promised to change. On this occasion she moved back with her parents, staying with them for about six weeks before moving to a rented home.

When Jamie tried to coax her back, she at first refused but according to her mother, Julie's resolve weakened when she was ill with the flu. 'Jamie came around with Lucozade and flowers. Soon she moved back.'

Soon after she returned, he had his first brush with the law and discovered the value of good legal advice. When he lost his licence for drink-driving he managed to claim victory from the humiliation by bragging how he beat the system. 'Even that was a farce. Jamie ran from the police and got into a bottle of whisky before the police could catch up with him,' Ray said. According to Patricia, 'When it came to court he had a good lawyer, who picked holes in the two policemen's statements. Julie went to court and pleaded for him. She was heavily pregnant with Matthew.' His licence was suspended for four months. 'When Julie went into labour, she had to drive herself to hospital.'

With busy lives and young children, Matthew and Samantha, who was born two years later, the Ramages started to rely on the Garretts as babysitters – a role the older couple embraced. But often they felt they were treated as unpaid domestic help rather than part of an extended family. After returning from taking the children to their caravan at Inverloch they were hurt when introduced to some of the Ramages upwardly-mobile friends. 'They were surprised to see Julie's family. It was as if we weren't spoken about,' Patricia said. 'Their friends would even ask if we were over on holiday.'

Their strained relationship effectively fractured after another alcohol-fuelled row in 1993. 'Jamie got more abusive as he drank more. He would sneer at everything that we held dear,' Patricia said. Jamie told Julie that her parents were not allowed to see the children at Christmas. Eventually he relented and said Patricia could see the kids as long as Ray wasn't home. So desperate was she to see her grandchildren that she took the day off work for the Ramage-sanctioned meeting. But Jamie's brittle indignation was tempered by the need for free childcare. '(For) the next three or four years we only saw the children when they wanted a babysitter. Julie was told by Jamie that she could stay for twenty minutes when she dropped off or picked up the kids,' Patricia said. Finally they were permitted to attend school plays and school sports. Jamie would not speak to them although he would occasionally favour them with a nod. They always sat behind the family, never with them.

Despite the bizarre rules, Jamie still had a serious problem with his father-in-law. 'He even told Julie that his ambition in life was to outlive me. I found this very odd considering that I am now 70.'

While the older man felt Ramage was clearly strange, he believed that at least he didn't play favourites. 'It wasn't just Pat and I – he treated everyone poorly.'

DOMESTIC violence is the socially homogenised term for wife bashing and child abuse. It is, we are often led to believe, something that happens amongst the poorly educated, the chronically unemployed and downtrodden. It is not supposed to happen in nice families, with picture postcard homes and kids in private schools. People with horses and imported cars and beach houses and smart friends, who talk about politics and the environment and their hopes for their children during pleasant dinner parties. Smart, independent women know there is no excuse for staying with wife beaters, men who apologise and cry and say it will never happen again. Until the next time.

Julie Ramage appeared to have the story-book home with the story-book life. The couple's double storey red clinker brick home, with white shutters on the windows, a well-manicured lawn, roses and well-clipped hedge bushes in a quiet court off Mont Albert Road could have been transplanted from the English county where they had met as teenagers. The worn basketball ring attached to the double garage showed it was a family home where kids could play in the street if they didn't want to wander to the park just a few hundred metres away. But like many things in the Ramage family the façade appeared to be more important than the reality. Downstairs the house was beautifully furnished. Upstairs it was a shell, like their marriage. Jamie like to drink good wines but kept the bottles in 'racks' made of cardboard supermarket carry boxes.

Gilda Pekin first met Julie Ramage at a Balwyn health centre when their sons were receiving their two-month check-ups. More than eighteen years later, they remained close friends. 'I was never really fond of Jamie as he was dominating of Julie and dismissive of women generally,' she told police. Twice in the early years she saw the signs of domestic violence when Julie arrived at the kindergarten with bruises and black eyes. Her suspicions were confirmed when Julie rang in February 1991 and asked her to come over. 'Julie told me that she was going to the plastic surgeon. She had two black eyes and a broken nose. She said she had walked into a door.' A week later she confessed that Jamie had head-butted her. Mrs Pekin urged her friend to move out. 'I told her if someone hits you, you leave. I couldn't understand why she wouldn't leave him. Jamie had a financial hold over her.'

But he didn't just physically dominate her. 'I recall when Julie was preparing for her thirtieth birthday party she purchased a black dress to wear. Jamie didn't like the dress, he thought it was too revealing. He went with her to take the dress back. He chose the dress that she wore. He would go to the hairdresser's with her and tell the hairdresser how to do her hair. Jamie would even decide what nail polish she would wear. He controlled Julie to every extent. I also felt that she wasn't permitted by Jamie to have an opinion on anything.'

His desire to control her meant that any independent activity was seen as a threat. He tried to stop her riding horses and pressured her to share his passion for golf. While her twin sister went to university Julie had cut her education short to follow Jamie to Australia. But years later she felt it was time to return to school to qualify to be a teacher herself. But according to friends, Jamie sabotaged her ambitions by placing endless and meaningless hurdles in her path. Gilda Pekin remembered vividly that, 'Jamie wouldn't allow the expenditure on babysitters … she missed classes. Jamie made it difficult.' When he agreed to be home so that she could attend lectures at Deakin University he would be late or not turn up at all. Despite good grades she eventually gave up.

One early January the women had lunch in Lorne and lost track of time, leaving Julie slightly late to meet Jamie at their holiday home for a golf date. Her reaction, bordering on panic, stuck with Mrs Pekin. 'She was distressed. She said that he'd kill her if she wasn't home in time … she seemed terrified. We were fifteen minutes late.' So concerned was her friend that she rang Julie twice to see that Jamie hadn't over-reacted. This time he remained calm. It appeared to be a storm in a porcelain teacup. Friends all found him dominating and her submissive. He increasingly found he needed her popularity to maintain a social life. A fellow member of the Hurstbridge Adult Riders Club, Annette Luckman, said Julie once told her that Jamie, 'had no friends and relied on her socially'.

While he needed her network he remained jealous, bad tempered, controlling and violent. Mrs Luckman said that as late as 2003 she saw Julie with a bruised face. 'A few of us were standing around and one of the group asked Julie how she got the black eye. She replied, "I hit it on a door, what do you think?"'

When the Ramages went to a riding club Christmas barbecue, members saw how she changed in her husband's company. One said Jamie was 'quite stuck-up – he didn't mix well and looked uncomfortable'. Julie appeared nervous, apprehensive, as if worried about what her volatile and indulged husband might do. She later confided to one fellow rider that she was deeply unhappy, complaining that while her husband gave her anything she wanted, he still tried to control her. 'She said that I wouldn't believe the temper that Jamie had. On a number of occasions she told me that he had a terrible, terrible temper. I told her that she shouldn't stay if he had such a temper, she should get out.'

Gillian Holding, a co-owner of the clothing business where Julie worked as a bookkeeper and computer networker, said staff would have a cheap lunch out once a week. Jamie tried to cut it back to once a month. When co-worker Joanne Mclean first met Julie's husband she found him charming but soon found him obsessive and frightening. 'If we were ever in a social situation Jamie would just stare at her and she couldn't talk to anyone. It was sick. She told me he demanded sex every morning, even if she didn't want to, he would do it. She hated it, she couldn't stand it. She just wanted to enjoy life, have a normal life – she just couldn't relax. She was frightened to leave. I felt that if she left Jamie she would have been in a lot of danger. I would tell her that he would kill her. I don't know why I felt this way.'

She told another fellow worker that her husband demanded sex every morning as his non-negotiable marital right. 'She said she felt like a piece of meat, she said that it felt like rape.'

After a fight in 2001 Julie left home and stayed overnight at her sister's. 'As usual Jamie came crawling back (and) wooed her back,' a friend said. Julie's mother said that after the 24-hour separation that, outwardly at least, Jamie appeared to try to change. 'He again was friendly and charming. He had made a complete turnaround. I did note that Julie was cool to him. I now know that she left him because he had thrown her out of bed. He threw her across the room.' Patricia was relieved that the relationship appeared to improve. 'Julie was allowed to come and visit us and was allowed to go horse riding. Jamie started to treat Julie better. He bought her a new car, she accompanied him on business trips, and the house was being renovated.'

But the balance of power in the relationship had altered. Julie was growing in confidence. She had friends and a future. Jamie had worked all his adult life building business to create wealth. Now the firm he co-owned, a bath restoration business, was on virtual auto-pilot. He would later confide that he was bored. A marriage counsellor wrote that Ramage said, 'The business ran itself and he would come home and annoy Julie.' They argued less – only because Julie tried to ignore being baited. But the passive approach came at a cost. 'Recently she had just been … agreeing with James instead of fighting, which built up hatred inside her,' according to one counsellor.

But Julie Ramage had reached the point of no return deciding the marriage was doomed. In May 2003 she told her parents she intended to leave Jamie but would wait until November so she wouldn't interrupt Matthew's Year 12 exams. But a month later she decided she could no longer wait and would leave when he next took a business trip. The reason Julie jumped five months earlier than planned was due to an argument between the two over their daughter, Samantha. The father was concerned about the 15-year-old girl. He was strict, and, it would emerge, violent with her. Samantha would later tell police that a year earlier he had given her a black eye. 'He hit or slapped me the wrong way across the face ... It wasn't like the worst time ... Dad had hit me before.'

One Friday Samantha was supposed to come straight home from school but was two hours late. The parents argued – Julie later told a friend Jamie said, 'How can she help it when she had a slut of a mother like you?' According to the friend, 'that was the thing that made her think, "That's it I'm out of here". She told me that after this he demanded sex. She said that she just lay there and didn't move, she had made up her mind that she was leaving.'

Jamie had a five-day business trip to Korea and was to leave on June 9. When he was gone, she would make her move. Unlike previous attempts she tried to set herself up in a way that would lessen her dependence on him. This time, she felt, there would be no way he could charm – or bully – her to return home. She transferred $100,000 from their joint account and bought new furniture for a small rented house. She was to tell her children before she informed her husband. Samantha decided to go with her, while Matthew wanted to stay with his father in their partially renovated Balwyn home.

But even while she was planning her move, she told her mother she feared Jamie would respond with violence. 'She expressed that she was frightened of Jamie. She also told us that she didn't want half of everything, just enough to buy a small house and for him to take care of the children's education.' 'I asked her if he had been violent towards her and then she reminded me of injuries that we thought were to do with horse riding or accidents ... I think she was still trying to hide the violence from us. When Julie was preparing to move, Ray and I offered to help her. She didn't want us to hire the van. She said she didn't want Jamie coming after us or killing her horse.'

Jamie was due home on Saturday so Julie moved out the day before on Black Friday, June 13, 2003. Ray went to the little house in Canberra Road, Toorak, she had rented. He fitted a bell to the front gate and checked all the locks. The father was not concerned with burglars but with her soon to be ex-husband. 'We were afraid of what Jamie would do when he found out she had left,' Patricia said.

When Jamie's plane touched down in Sydney, he rang his wife to give her time to pick him up from Melbourne airport. That's when she broke the news that their marriage was over. In a note left for him at home she wrote, 'I know that you would really try to do anything to keep us together but that is not the point because it's what is truly in your heart that matters and I know that you can't help yourself and the real you bubbles to the surface and I don't like that person ... If you said I could do anything I wanted I couldn't because I have been conditioned over the years to always worry about your reaction. If you do care for me please let me go without a horrible fight for the kids' sake ... I could hate you so much for some of the things you have done and said to me over the years but I also understand that you are a good person and that you work hard and most importantly that you love our kids very much ... Please talk to your friends and think things through before going crazy … I have tried to leave the house clean and tidy and prepared a meal for this evening. Take care, Julie.'

Jamie didn't go crazy – at least not initially. He began a campaign to woo her back. He wanted to show her that he could change and be the man she wanted.

The life-long conservative took to meditation, sent her flowers, tried counselling, opened up to her friends and continued to renovate their home. He had stared down near bankruptcy when one of his companies had threatened to capsize, fought through marriage problems for years and had kept his family together. He was not the type to give up – at least not without a fight.

He rang Julie's mother and while he acknowledged that the Garretts owed him nothing, he pleaded for advice. 'He was very calm and said that he wasn't going to react as people expected him to.' Ray Garrett was not the type to offer false hope or fake friendship. He told him he should get on with life. 'I told him he was a good-looking man with money and he could find someone else.' Julie told friends she knew he could not alter his basic personality although she was pleasantly surprised that Jamie was trying to control his notorious temper.

Even though she knew the marriage was over, she did not try to sever all ties. They would meet about twice a week for an occasional meal but Julie was sufficiently wary of her husband's black side to make sure the meetings were always in public. Her mother said, 'Julie was happy. She laughed like she used to laugh, and we had our happy daughter back. She told me that Jamie was being very reasonable and that she wanted to help him. She told me he was having counselling, but not that it was for anger management. She hoped it would help him for any future relationships he may have. She only wished him well.' Another friend said Julie wanted 'to ease him out slowly.

He thought they would get back together. She wanted to stay friends for the kids' sake.'

Jamie Ramage chopped and changed counsellors. As always, the driven businessman wanted results and did not appear impressed when told of his own failings. He grilled her friends. He told them he knew he had been too dominating and he wished he could turn the clock back. But it was too late – while he was looking back, for the first time in years his wife was looking forward.

An office worker friend said, 'She was happy she could go out and have a drink. One Friday night we went to the Botanical Hotel, Julie was actually shaking because she was nervous. She told me that she had never done it, never gone to a bar by herself. Jamie would never allow it.' She was introduced to a friend of her twin sister's who shared her love of horses. Laurence Webb was physically imposing like her husband but that would appear to be the only similarity.

Webb had been a successful businessman who was between jobs. He was a poetry-reading, theatre lover who Julie found fascinating. They soon began to go out.

On the evening of Friday, July 18, Julie told her mother she was going with Jamie to watch Matthew play football for Scotch College at Geelong the following day. 'I was horrified and warned her not to go anywhere other than a public place with him. Julie told me that she wasn't silly and wouldn't do such a thing.'

During the football they talked. It was then she told him she had met someone else. Shocked, hurt and feeling betrayed Jamie listened. The next day he contacted one of her friends who was being worn down by his stream of needy calls. This time however she was struck by his calmness. 'He asked me how I thought he should deal with it. He asked me if I thought he should wait until she got sick of him or it passed. He didn't seem upset. I was impressed that he had taken it in his stride.'

While he continued to talk to friends, Julie spent the days with her new boyfriend. On the Sunday she told her mother she'd had a blissful day. 'She told me she had been horse riding, Laurence had read her some poetry and she had some wine at the pub. She said it was all she ever wanted.'

The next day she was dead.

JULIE RAMAGE was happier than she had been for years when she agreed to meet Jamie at their partially renovated Balwyn home for lunch that Monday. Almost certainly she expected the builder to be there and had no intention of being alone with her estranged husband. One friend would recall later she was told the separated couple planned to meet the builder that week to inspect the work that had begun nearly five months earlier. But Jamie Ramage had told the builder to knock off for the day because he wanted to be alone with his wife. It is likely he wanted to impress her with the renovations as part of his plan to get her to return.

That morning Ramage dropped his son at Scotch College for a football recovery session at 7.15am and then swung his green Jaguar towards his business in Collingwood. Staff said he appeared tense and distracted during the morning. A fellow worker remembered trying to joke him out of his mood. 'He snapped at me, he didn't see the humour in what I was saying. This was unusual for James.' He told her he was going out that day because he had a 'meeting with the renovators'. He left, bought rolls for lunch and arrived home around 11.40am.

That morning Julie drove Samantha to Lauriston Girls School in her silver Mini before driving to work at Glenferrie Road, Hawthorn. She was making morning coffee when she saw a friend in the kitchen and announced, 'I'm on cloud nine'. She said she had told Jamie about her new boyfriend because she wanted 'everything out in the open'. At 12.10pm she headed out for lunch, leaving her office heater and computer on. No-one expected her to be long as she had a meeting with her boss scheduled for early afternoon.

Carpenter Graeme McIntosh arrived at the Marock Place house at 7.45am to work through the day but Ramage rang to say Julie would be coming around and he should leave by 11.40am.

Ramage asked him not to leave a mess and said he would be paid for a full day. The builder offered to come back after lunch and if Julie's car was not there he would continue working. 'He told me no, he insisted that I take the day off.'

Ramage moved a table from the laundry into the family room and began to prepare lunch. Julie arrived around midday dressed in blue jodhpur pants, blue jumper, black jacket and R.M. Williams boots. What happened in the next 30 minutes before Ramage beat and then strangled his wife to death will never be known as only one self-serving version can be recorded.

According to Ramage his wife was off-handed and cold. She dismissed him, swore, taunted him and demeaned him sexually. Julie Ramage was 172 centimetres tall and weighed 67 kilos. Her husband was around 185 centimetres and weighed nearly 95 kilos. He was an ex-rugby player who kept fit playing touch football, bike riding and rowing. He had previously beaten her, head-butted her, broken her nose, thrown her from bed, demanded non-consensual sex and repeatedly bullied and intimidated her. She had told friends and family she did not want to be alone with him because of fears for her safety. She had said she wanted to ease out of the relationship, that she didn't want their separation to be poisoned with bitterness and urged him not to go crazy. Yet on this rainy, cold day, when there were no independent witnesses, Ramage says his wife went out of her way to belittle and hurt him.

According to his uncontested version he showed Julie the renovations and she seemed unimpressed. When he tried to tell her how hard he and Matthew had worked she was insulting and dismissive. He said that when he told her of the difficulties of keeping going, 'she sort of made this sort of, you know, wank wank sort of sign'. He claimed she said he should have renovated the house years earlier as 'you had enough money … that hurt a lot'.

He would tell police that as they sat down, 'I just pleaded with her, "What do I have to do? What, what can I do?" And she sort of said, "You don't get it, do you? I'm over you. I should have left you ten years ago".'

When he asked about Samantha, he claimed she said, 'It's none of your fucking business. I'm not with you any more'. This from a woman who had earlier written to him pleading that their break-up should be civilised for the sake of the children. He claims he then asked about her relationship with Webb and she allegedly responded, 'I've had sleepovers with him'. Ramage said, 'That really, really hurt.'

She was then supposed to have said how much nicer he was, 'and you know he rides horses and cares for her more and all that sort of stuff'. Ramage claimed she said sex with Webb was better and sex with Jamie 'repulses me' then screwed up her face in disgust. In his confession he claims she then moved to end the conversation, 'and that's when I lost it. As she stood up, I … I stood up and hit her and then I just wanted it to stop and that's when I strangled her and you don't know how much I wish I could change that.'

EXPERIENCED homicide investigators say when a man kills his wife in a flash of murderous rage he usually rings the police or a friend to confess. One said that in 75 per cent of cases the offender is waiting for police at the scene when they arrive. Filled with grief and remorse he tells his story and is repulsed by his own actions. But Ramage was not that type. No matter what he would later say, his first, strongest and driving motivation was self-preservation. He told police he thought, 'I might as well just call someone'. But he didn't.

He did not check her pulse, he did not check her breathing, he did not attempt to revive her and he did not call an ambulance. Police say she may still have been alive although it is impossible to tell. James Stuart Ramage, father, husband and killer felt there was only one person worth saving and that was himself. He would spend the rest of the day in a cold-blooded attempt to conceal the crime.

At 12.38 he rang his plumber, Patrick Leonard, and told him not to come to the house that day. He then dragged his wife's body out the back door into the double garage and into the boot of his Jag making sure to place her on a sheet to minimise any DNA contamination. He filled a red bucket from the laundry with warm soapy water and used blue and white tea towels to mop up the blood. He changed from his dark blue jumper and chino pants because of blood droplets then drove her Mini to the rear car park of Colombos, a large pizza restaurant in Whitehorse Road, before walking the 700 metres home.

He rang his work to say he would not be back that afternoon, grabbed a shovel and drove to Kinglake. Supposedly distraught by what he had done, he was still cool enough to try and build an alibi on the run by twice ringing his wife's mobile phone that he knew was in her handbag in his car. He knew that when she was reported missing, police would trace her to his house. He would then say she had left and would have phone records to suggest he had tried to contact her later in the day. He dug two shallow holes in the bush, leaving the body in one and his compromised clothing, towels, sheets and her handbag containing $51.15, phone, licence and a bank cheque for $194 in the other. He left, bought petrol and tried to conceal any forensic evidence by running the Jag through the car wash at the Diamond Creek BP service station.

That afternoon he was due to check a piece of imported granite specially ordered for the kitchen renovations from a firm in Reservoir. Less than three hours after killing his wife Ramage wandered into the factory to keep his appointment. According to the manager of Acropolis Marble and Granite, Lena Tzimas-Kori, Ramage was, 'very well-mannered and polite. He was very cool. He did not seem stressed to me'. There was only one moment when he showed any sign of being distracted. He removed one of his Blundstone boots to rearrange an annoying blue sock that was rubbing on his foot. He left after ten minutes and drove home. He washed his second set of clothes and had a bath.

Around 5.45pm Samantha grew impatient waiting for her mother to pick her up from school and caught a tram to their rented Toorak home. Matthew arrived home in Balwyn. His father said he couldn't be bothered cooking and took his son out for dinner. He drove the Jag and parked out the front of Colombos. As the pair sat and chatted about their goals in life, Jamie Ramage knew that his dead wife's car was still sitting twenty metres away in the rear car park. Police speculate Ramage chose the restaurant as a twisted show of domination against his dead wife. He paid the $35 bill with his gold Visa card that had a $30,000 credit limit, then took his son home

At 7.30pm, Samantha rang her father and asked if he knew

where Julie was. He responded she was 'probably off with that Laurence bloke or something'. But Ramage was smart enough to know that it was only a matter of time before his wife was reported missing and that he would soon be interviewed as a murder suspect. Certainly when Julie's sister Jane was told, she immediately feared that Ramage had killed her.

He decided he needed help and called in an old family friend for advice. It proved to be an inspired choice – the friend was one of Australia's best criminal barristers, Dyson Hore-Lacy QC. They met nearby at the Harp Hotel in Kew. When he told the barrister what he had done, Hore-Lacy called in experienced solicitor Steve Pica. The three men talked. The hotel video shows the men in deep conference. Whatever was said remains between them but when Ramage and Pica crossed the road to walk into the foyer of the Boroondara police station the cool businessman was ready to give his version of events.

NOTHING destroys confidence and self-esteem like a visit to the homicide squad interview room. But Jamie Ramage doesn't look like a man at the point of breaking as he sits across a small table chatting to police about how he killed his wife the day before. Dressed in the casual attire of the successful business-man on a day off, he talks quietly as he explains matter-of-factly the details of the killing. Earlier he took police to the gravesite where he had 'stupidly buried Julie'. He tells police he tried to patch their marriage using Romance 101. 'I've written her letters. I've sent her CDs. I've sent her roses. I've sent her all that sort of thing.'

In answer to question 386, he says. 'That's all I can say. I mean I regret it. I wish I could go back. I wish I could turn back the clock. I wish I could … I could change it. I … I don't understand … I mean, doing … taking her up to Kinglake and all that. It's just stupid.' He wished for a lot of things that day in the homicide squad interview room. But there was one thing he didn't wish – that Julie Ramage was still alive.

RAMAGE was charged with murder but the jury later convicted him of the lesser offence of manslaughter, accepting that he acted under provocation. This meant that while he knew what he was doing was wrong his ability to control his actions was somehow mitigated because of the behaviour of the victim. In other words Julie Ramage was somehow partially to blame for her own death. The jury had to rely heavily on Ramage's version of what happened in the Balwyn house just before he killed his wife. His self-serving confession, delivered to the homicide squad just hours after he spoke to experienced defence lawyers in the Harp Hotel would prove to be an almost text-book provocation defence. So good in fact, it could have been used in law lectures to budding barristers.

The verdict of manslaughter due to provocation created outrage in the community. Many failed to understand how a wife, who had previously been subjected to domestic violence could somehow be considered to have inflamed her husband to such a point that it provided legal mitigation for his decision to kill her. It was not as though he had walked into a bedroom and found his wife having an affair. It was not as though she had a history of baiting or humiliating him. It was not as though she was threatening him with financial ruin or with running away with their children. Like tens of thousands of people she decided to leave her partner. She was attempting to make the best of a difficult but not impossible situation. That's it.

She tried to leave in a dignified manner and with concerns for her husband and children. But she was not about to contest Ramage's version of what was said in the partially renovated home which led an intelligent and rational man to strangle her to death with his bare hands. Many serious legal minds were clearly uncomfortable with the law as it stood.

In sentencing Ramage on December 9, 2004, Justice Robert Osborn said: *I of course must apply the current law whatever view I may hold as to the desirability of change to it*. He said he was *satisfied the killing was deliberate and done with murderous intent; the killing was brutal involving an overwhelming and continuing assault on a smaller and weaker victim* (and) *this was not a case of objectively extreme provocation*. He also said: *I am not persuaded you have expressed real remorse for the killing; and the killing of which you are guilty was of a type which attacks the foundations of relationships within our society and must be the subject of general deterrence. After the fatal assault you made no attempt to revive your wife or to obtain emergency assistance for her. Rather, you embarked immediately on a sequence of careful and calculated actions to try and cover up what you had done. I have no doubt that you feel regret for your actions and the consequential disintegration of your former way of life, but I am not persuaded you have felt or expressed genuine remorse for the brutal killing of your wife and the abrupt termination of her life when she had much to look forward to*.

He sentenced Ramage to eleven years with a minimum of eight.

AFTER his arrest Ramage was moved to another red brick building – the Melbourne Assessment Prison. For a man new to the jail system he appeared to adjust quickly. In a letter to a friend he wrote, 'Well, life has changed a great deal for me. Apart from dealing with what I have done I also have to deal with living in here. The violence etc I think is a little exagger-

ated. As long as you stay away from the
to be OK. A little like the playground. Th
quite interesting characters in here. Apart fr
office I also am talking to some of the young
where I can.'

Police wanted to seize the Jaguar he used to transp
body of his dead wife to the bush before he buried her but
Office of Public Prosecutions decided not to pursue the claim.
Lawyers said his assets had been handed to his children and
they did not want to compound the crime by hounding the
innocent. Within weeks of the sentencing the Victorian state
government announced it would reform the law so that such a
defence could not be mounted again. Acting Premier John
Thwaites said: 'Provocation does tend to lend to a culture
where the victim is blamed rather than the perpetrator.

The partial defence of provocation was developed when the
offence of murder carried the mandatory death penalty It also
harks back to an era when it was acceptable, especially for men,
to have a violent response to an alleged breach of a person's
honour.'

Attorney-General Rob Hulls said, when making the
announcement that he had received 2500 letters calling for the
reform of the defence of provocation after the Ramage case: 'In
future, this defence will not be available'. He said for too long
the law of provocation had allowed killers to 'get away with
murder'.

Many believe one of those is James Ramage.

troublemakers it seems
ere's actually some
om a job in the
guys helping

ort the
the

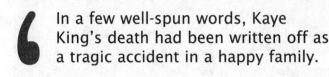

In a few well-spun words, Kaye King's death had been written off as a tragic accident in a happy family.

5.
AN OPEN CASE

IT was her boots he saw first – new blue gumboots with bright orange soles, as shiny and clean as they had been when she brought them home from town the previous week. They were sticking out, soles upward, from a brick-lined pit built years before to drain effluent from the old pig pens nearby.

Earlier, driving home to the farm with his father and younger brother, 16-year-old Peter King had sensed something wrong, the way children and pets often do. Now, despite his unease, the meaning of the scene still took a moment to sink in. For a heartbeat, he thought only that the boots looked strangely out of place.

Then he saw legs in the boots, and knew. His mother was upside down in the foul water, hidden by long grass and a ramshackle fence.

He screamed to his father and brother. 'I couldn't move,' he was to say later of the few seconds that shattered his life. 'Dad and John started to run over. Dad grabbed hold of her and helped me lift her out.'

Peter gave his mother mouth-to-mouth resuscitation. He did it fiercely for what 'seemed like an hour' but might have been ten minutes. Dirty water regurgitated from her throat. For a second his heart leapt because he thought it meant she had started breathing, but the feeling was replaced by dread. 'She felt so cold,' he mumbles all these years later, reliving a scene that still makes him thrash and cry out in his sleep. 'I'd never felt anyone so cold before.' The boy needed a miracle but he didn't get one.

Nancy Kaye King, farmer's wife, churchgoer, and mother of four, was dead at 38. It was just before 3pm on a wet winter Tuesday – June 25, 1991.

SOME things stand out in the two boys' memories of that nightmarish afternoon. John, the younger of the brothers, ran the 100 or so metres to the house to the telephone.

He called Heather Hosie, one of his mother's best friends, whose husband Ron was also a dairy farmer and Ayrshire cattle breeder, like the Kings. ('John was screaming at me over the phone,' Heather was to recall recently, lip trembling at the memory.) The shocked boy then called an ambulance. The Hosies lived close by and Heather got there fast. She found John madly telephoning everyone he could think of. She took the handpiece from him, led him out and took him to the highway turn-off to wait for the ambulance and guide it in to the farm. She was already dreading the thought of having to meet to break the news to Nicole, Kaye's youngest, who was a few days off her thirteenth birthday.

Meanwhile Peter left his mother's body and ran to the house

to telephone another neighbour, Pam Malcolm, at whose home he and John had stayed the previous night. He made other calls, too, to neighbours and relatives. Then he tried to resuscitate his mother again.

The ambulance came at 3.18pm. The grim-faced officers went through the motions with oxygen bottles and mask, mainly to comfort the boys. But they already knew it was a job for the undertaker – and the law. One called base to notify the police.

Two young uniformed constables arrived from Shepparton in the divisional van just before 4pm. They looked at the body, spoke to the 'ambos' then picked their way through the churned-up mud and manure to the house to see the dead woman's husband, Graeme King.

The policemen were sympathetic. Sport was the glue that held the district together and the Kings loved their sport and were known for it. The policemen recognised the tall, dark farmer with the 'Newk' moustache as a local football club identity and 'good bloke'. He was already surrounded by neighbours in the kitchen. The big man was too 'visibly distressed' to say much, one constable noted later, but he managed to say his wife must have stumbled – or been knocked over by cattle – while moving cows from around the haystack while he was away from the farm, picking up the boys from a friend's place.

The story was repeated as more neighbours, friends and relatives arrived. It seemed a plausible explanation for a tragic death – enough, anyway, that although other details were to fade from memory. Years later, both policemen confidently recalled it as a freak accident caused by cattle knocking the woman into a 'well'.

Which was strange, because not everyone subscribed to the cow theory, even on the night.

When Ken Mansell heard about the 'drowning' on the police radio, he knew he would be called to the scene, near Katandra, twenty kilometres north-east of Shepparton.

Mansell, a local detective sergeant for years, knew the police department had a policy of sending crime investigators to check apparent suicides and fatal accidents, and he knew why. Someone upstairs was wary of potentially embarrassing mistakes following a couple of strange cases in which police had dismissed suspicious deaths as suicides.

A drover's son, Mansell knew about farms and cattle. Driving to the scene, he calculated the odds against an adult accidentally drowning in a well. Farms are dangerous, but most deaths on them are caused by machinery – tractors, post-hole diggers, motorbikes, grain augers – or falling from horses or in shooting accidents. 'Little kids drown on farms,' Mansell was to say later, 'but not adults – unless they *want* to drown themselves.'

Nothing he found out then or later was to persuade him Kaye King wanted to drown herself. Even if she had, she surely would have chosen the clean water in the irrigation channel, or a farm dam, both closer to the house.

Mansell reached the farm just before dark. Drizzle was falling from a sullen sky, the yard was jammed with mud-spattered cars and the worn weatherboard house was filling fast.

The Kings' teenage boys – Peter, John and older brother Jason – all played football for Katandra. Their father Graeme was vice-president of the football club and drank with the men who ran the game in the Goulburn Valley – a group that included some local police – while their mother was a popular volunteer in sport and community groups and the local Catholic church, always toiling behind the scenes. Now the district was rallying behind its own, with food and drink and sympathy.

When Mansell saw Kaye King's body lying beside the pit, it

was covered with hessian cow rugs. The pit was small – little more than a metre square – and separated from the lane and nearby haystack by a surrounding fence with an electric 'hot wire', which had been taken down on one side before the body was discovered. There was no obvious reason for anyone to go near the pit, which was usually dry but had about a metre of stagnant water in it after prolonged wet weather.

A sodden parka was lying next to the body. In the dying light, Mansell could see two things: the circular bruise on the dead woman's forehead – and that her gumboots were clean.

He ordered the pit be taped off and guarded, and called for the police surgeon, the homicide squad and crime scene analysts. He walked to the house. The mud ruined his brown leather brogues.

Mansell stood at the door and looked into the crowded kitchen. Most were lost in the drama of the moment and oblivious to him, but one person was looking back at him: the stricken husband, Graeme King.

'He watched me like a hawk,' Mansell was to recall. 'He didn't want anything to do with me.'

Mansell wasn't the only one with concerns.

Henry Wells, who lived (and still does) on a farm nearby, was president of the local football league and knew the Kings well. He was also a veteran policeman and was stationed at Cobram, further north. When he heard the news he drove straight to the Kings', still in uniform. He was dismayed by what he found. 'It was in full swing. The whole footy club crowd was there and the scene (in the house) was being treated as if it was no more than a car accident.'

Wells – who read the eulogy at the funeral a week later – was in a difficult position. He told Mansell of misgivings about Kaye's welfare. Graeme King was a heavy drinker with money problems and there were rumours of domestic strife. (The same, of course, might have been true of other battling farmers in the surrounding district, a point Mansell included in the statement he later made for the coroner.)

By this time the boys, Peter and John, had been separated and formally interviewed but their father had not. Mansell asked a detective to take a statement from King but he returned empty-handed, saying the farmer was too upset to speak coherently.

Mansell checked the boys' halting statements and compared notes with Wells. It didn't ease their minds. King had seemed anxious about Kaye's apparent absence as soon as he got home, and had sent the boys to look for her while he rushed to start milking much earlier than usual.

Kaye's friends talked about it later. One of them, Heather Hosie, wondered why King had rung her about 2.30pm that day to ask if Kaye was with her.

The homicide crew arrived from Melbourne just before 11pm. Graeme Collins, a detective constable with a bright future, began taking detailed notes, eventually filling 16 pages of foolscap. On top of one page he wrote in what might have been veiled exasperation: '100 people at house since notification'. He abbreviated Wells' and Mansell's comments as follows:

Wells: Cows. 2.30pm terribly early to milk them – very uncommon to do it.

Mansell: No reason for deceased to go into area where found.

Wells: Husband drinking a lot of heavy beer. Since being on light not as bad. Marriage under strain as result of drinking and financial strain. Deceased has confided in others ... Husband hot-tempered.

Collins made plenty more notes that night, a cryptic record of the ugly scene lit by the harsh emergency lights. The pretty woman who had been dancing at a debutante ball the previous

Friday night was now a cold, half-naked corpse lying in the chilly air with insects crawling over her skin, just another sad job for men who saw too many bad endings.

Later, Graeme King would say he hadn't noticed any bruises when hauling Kaye's body out of the pit. Others did.

As the technicians' cameras whirred and clicked to record the scene under the harsh emergency lights, Collins listed the 'oval-shaped dent' on her forehead, the nasty double bruise around the left nipple, the abrasions on her ribs and belly, and below one knee. And the torn, bruised hands and broken fingernails, which had been unmarked at the debutante ball and football club dinner she'd attended the weekend before. Kaye's friends always admired the way she kept her nails so nicely despite working around the farm. But something had knocked them around in the last few hours of her life.

Had she hurt her fingers struggling to climb out of the pit – or struggling in some way before she got there? It was not the only unanswered question.

Collins wrote, 'No mud or dirt on boots', then underlined it and added the words, 'track leading to scene extremely muddy and wet'.

It was after 1am before the government undertaker finally took the body for the long trip to the state coroner's morgue in Melbourne. A tired uniformed policeman went with him, and ensured the body was locked in the 'homicide fridge' at 3.25am.

At that stage, foul play was suspected until proven otherwise.

But the head of the homicide crew, the impeccably dressed Senior Sergeant Charlie Bezzina, had a problem worse than sodden shoes and muddy trousers. If it were homicide, the actual crime scene might not be the neatly taped-off section around the pit – but in the house, which had been filled with people for hours. Any evidence there would be destroyed or hopelessly compromised. He must have hoped the autopsy would produce a smoking gun – a clear piece of evidence to prove an offence beyond reasonable doubt. It wasn't to be. A policeman's lot is not a happy one.

JUST after noon on the day his mother died, Jason King tried to call her for their regular lunchtime chat. Jason was an apprentice signwriter with Telecom in Melbourne. He called on Tuesdays and Thursdays and Kaye always answered. So when the call rang out, he was uneasy; he knew they had plenty to talk about.

Jason, then 18, had always been close to his mother. He had become a confidant as her marriage soured, hearing things she hid from all but her closest friends. Their talks had become more intense in previous weeks because Kaye was preparing to leave Jason's father, an escape that poverty and her Catholic beliefs had blocked in the past. Now she had a motive to leave – and the means to do it.

For some time, Kaye had suspected Graeme of having an affair. Now she knew with whom. She had told Jason – and her women friends – that he had taunted her, leaving the house late at night to see the other woman. Kaye had found out it was a divorcee Graeme had known for years through showing stud cattle. It was messy, humiliating, and grounds for separation.

Jason had urged her to leave, as had her friends Sharon Canobie, Heather Hosie and Pam Burgmann. But Kaye had been worried about Nicole, her youngest child, and vacillated between leaving immediately and waiting until her daughter was older. At last, though, she had the money to support herself when she did leave.

Seven years earlier, her left hand had been injured in a road accident. A series of operations had left the hand stiff and disfigured, though not affecting the power of her upper arm. After a drawn-out compensation case, after all legal expenses were paid, she had finally got about $60,000. Not as much as she'd hoped – but enough to set her up in her home town of Kyneton, where her father and two of her four brothers lived.

But $60,000 was also what it would take to get the Kings 'out of the red' – to clear debts racked up when interest rates of up to 25 per cent hit the farm in the late 1980s. If she left and took her money with her, it would leave Graeme stranded.

Kaye's elderly father and her only sister, Judith, had visited that weekend to see Peter partner Heather Hosie's daughter at a debutante ball, and Jason had wanted his mother to return to Kyneton with Judith. But Judith had her own children with her and her car was almost full – and Kaye did not want to leave Nicole behind. She decided to stay a few more days.

Jason was still working in the signwriting workshop when he got the news, some time after 3.30pm. His supervisor took the message.

'I watched his face drain white,' Jason said later. 'He hung up and said, "Sit down, I've got something to tell you. Your mum's had an accident on the farm and passed away".'

Someone called Jason's friend Luke, an apprentice carpenter. They drove north, too fast, in Jason's HQ Holden. After trying the Shepparton Hospital, expecting to find the family at his mother's deathbed, they got to the farm after dark.

'The whole place was lit up like a circus,' Jason said later. 'Everybody was inside. When I went in I walked up to my father and said, "What the fuck's gone on here?"'

NOT all love stories end in tragedy, but a tragedy may begin as a love story. The events that led Kaye to the farm at Katandra began twenty years before, in the town of Kyneton, between

Melbourne and Bendigo. Kaye, named Nancy after her mother but always known by her second name, was one of six children of a house painter called Jim Thompson, whose sons still run the family business there.

Kaye was quiet and respectable but she turned heads. Class photographs from Kyneton's Sacred Heart Convent show a strikingly pretty girl. She left school at 15 to care for her ill mother and later worked at a local supermarket. At 18, she was all long hair and miniskirts, a shy entrant in the local Miss Showgirl competition. Industrious and kind but not fired by ambition, she was marked for early marriage and motherhood as soon as she found Mr Right.

Kaye's brother Ian played football for the nearby Bacchus Marsh team; one weekend in 1971 he took his kid sister to a team-mate's engagement party. She caught the eye of two Bacchus Marsh boys but it was the tall, dark farmer's son, Graeme King, who gave her his telephone number. Kaye called and wrote to him, and he drove his old Holden over to see her at weekends. He was her first boyfriend. They were engaged in mid-1972 and had to bring the wedding forward when she fell pregnant soon after. Her father sat in his car and sobbed when she told him.

Graeme was the third of six sons born to Ray and Eileen King, who farmed near Bacchus Marsh before moving to Katandra in 1973. Graeme was a good young footballer until the last game of the 1969 season, when a tough former VFL player elbowed him in the temple. He went to Royal Melbourne Hospital with concussion, a fractured skull and a ruptured eardrum, but it was two blood clots on his brain that worried the surgeons.

King never played again. He was 190 centimetres tall, strong and athletic and only 18. St Kilda Football Club had approached him just before the injury and he thought he would get to play alongside the famous 'Big Carl' Ditterich at St Kilda. Some sensed in him later the discontent of a man who could have been a contender. He certainly had a temper. Whether it was the effect of the brain injury or in his nature no one was sure, but most who knew him didn't fancy crossing him.

When Graeme's parents and three younger brothers moved to the irrigation farm at Katandra, the newlyweds went too – patching up a run-down house on the property to live in before buying their own smaller farm nearby in 1977. By that time, they had three sons under four years and Nicole on the way.

Graeme and Kaye King looked good in public. They cut a dash around country shows with the stud Ayrshire cattle they started breeding in 1981. Their children were good-looking and excelled at sport.

But beneath the surface there was plenty of trouble and not much money.

Kaye told friends that her father-in-law – a big, handsome, dominating figure – had once propositioned her. She suspected Graeme also had a roving eye. When the children were small, Kaye's sister Judith recalls, she took them and left him for a few weeks – staying with her parents until he begged her to come home.

Time didn't mend his ways and alcohol inflamed them. Kaye said little, but family and friends suspected Graeme was violent. During a trivial argument at a family barbecue, Graeme throttled Kaye's brother-in-law to the floor. Kaye was close to her sister, but Judith and her husband hardly visited the Kings after that. Much later, at Merimbula, Graeme would also attack his youngest brother, Noel. His own children grew up nervous of him.

KAYE King had been dead 24 hours, give or take, when a forensic pathologist and a mortuary technician slid her body onto a steel table and started work.

Dr Shelley Robertson had done 'about a thousand' autopsies – many of them homicides and suicides – and has done thousands more since. All but a few are a blur to her. But the King case would stick in her mind because of the circumstances, the nature and number of the injuries – and the investigation.

No one injury Kaye suffered could have caused death. The odd thing was that there were so many of them in so many different places. Robertson noted fifteen surface bruises and abrasions divided between the face, torso and hands. Any one group of them might have come from a simple fall – but all of them?

They were the sort of 'trivial' injuries people get in pub brawls. There was more. Robertson peeled back the skin on the right side of the neck and found a subcutaneous bruise in the hollow spot above the collar bone – right where a thumb would press if the deceased had been grabbed around the throat. And an unlikely spot to be hurt in a fall.

The pathologist judged that the bruise on the forehead came from a blow perhaps hard enough to knock the victim unconscious, but not hard enough to kill. Death came after she went headfirst into the water. Under 'cause of death' in the notes Robertson made, she wrote 'unascertainable'. This did not mean 'accidental' or 'not suspicious', a point she thought would be clear to a waiting homicide detective that day. It was certainly implied in her formal report, which stated: 'While blood-stained fluid in airways and pulmonary haemorrhages are suggestive of drowning, the reasons for failure by the deceased to extricate herself from the well are not clear given the lack of underlying medical conditions, negative toxicological analysis and trivial nature of other injuries.'

In the careful scientific terms of an expert routinely cross-examined about her conclusions in court, Robertson had left the door open for investigation.

Kaye King hadn't been shot, poisoned or bashed to death – but neither was she ill, drunk, drugged or injured enough to drown accidentally in something hardly bigger than a hotel spa. If she was unconscious when she went into the water, why was she? And if she wasn't unconscious, why couldn't she climb out?

These were the questions the autopsy posed. Somehow they were lost in translation.

From when Ken Mansell reached the scene the night before, the death had been treated as suspicious. No effort was spared in the first 24 hours. The police helicopter came to get aerial shots. Crime scene surveyors were booked to survey the scene.

But the moment the pathologist's notes were relayed to the investigators, the case folded. They cancelled the surveyors, handed the job back to the local police and left. 'It became "accidental" overnight,' says Mansell, shaking his head.

Asked about this fourteen years later, one of the former homicide detectives offers a theory that Kaye King might have hit her head on a wooden fence post, then swallow-dived into the pit and drowned. Another former detective recalls a variation of this theme – that she had hit herself on a steel 'star picket' after tripping over a low fence wire and falling in the pit. Either way, they suggest, the fence did it – with or without help from a careless cow.

The fact was someone decided the autopsy result wasn't enough to justify investigating the circumstances. One of the ex-homicide detectives cites an old squad adage: 'We're not the almost-homicide squad.'

If forensics couldn't nail a killer, forget it.

It was a suddenly popular view on that Wednesday afternoon. Within hours of the autopsy, someone briefed the media and killed the story. Next day the *Herald Sun* ran a paragraph stating: 'Homicide detectives have ruled out foul play in the death of a woman who fell into a well near Shepparton.' The *Shepparton News* and local television and radio ran the same angle. In a few well-spun words, Kaye King's death had been written off as a tragic accident in a happy family.

Yet, reading the pathology report, it would have been just as reasonable to conclude that foul play could *not* be ruled out. The only fact that mattered was that a woman's battered body had been found in a shallow pit. How she got there was still a matter of conjecture. Context was everything.

When the homicide squad dropped the ball, Ken Mansell lost heart. He interviewed the woman with whom Graeme King had been having the affair before – and after – Kaye's death, but she said little on the record. And, three months later, Mansell finally got King to make the statement he should have made on the first day. He sensed the younger King boys, then aged sixteen and fifteen, were scared of their father and had not been frank in their police statements about the state of their parents' marriage. Because Jason had not been present on the day, he was not interviewed at all.

In any case, the guarded forensic pathology report was enough to throw doubt on the 'accident' scenario. When the inquest was finally held at Shepparton in early 1993, a coroner swiftly made an open finding: in other words, he could not rule that Kaye King's death was accidental, nor that anyone had killed her.

Mansell prepared the brief and gave evidence. Afterwards, King approached him in the court lobby and demanded to know if the open finding would affect his 'insurance'. The detective assumed he was talking about the $60,000 compensation Kaye got before her death, and was angry that King was talking about money. There was a heated exchange. They haven't spoken to each other since, but Mansell has never stopped wondering about what happened to Kaye King.

Without Kaye, and with the spectre of her death hanging over them, the King family fell apart. Peter and John were the worst: they smoked, drank and brawled as if they had a death wish.

Graeme King's relationship with the other woman didn't last. For all the faults the King children and others saw in her, she was a hard worker who ran good farms, she stood to inherit property and money, and she was shrewd. Meanwhile, as King's ordinary little farm went from rundown to worse, she heard the rumours and wondered about her chances of future happiness.

She came in from milking one evening to find King watching television and drinking, waiting for her to cook for him. She glimpsed the future and ended the relationship. Later, he was to propose marriage to two other women, but both reneged. One, a Camden cattle breeder, saw red when he offered her his dead wife's engagement ring.

King sold his farm and cattle and rented a farmhouse until he bought a small property at Stanhope – on the other side of Shepparton from Katandra. As a fresh start, it wasn't a wild success. He built up another Ayrshire herd, but the stud cattle scene was small and rumours dogged him. He sold up again, moved into an empty shop in Stanhope, started labouring for a tomato farmer and spent his money on beer and solo trips to Bali. And he rarely talked about his wife, even less about her death – especially to his children.

Jason moved to Sydney in 1998 and buried himself in a new

world, but he couldn't bury the past. His brothers, meanwhile, were haunted by what happened the day their mother died, and still trapped in a love-hate relationship with a father they feared. Like him, they drank a lot and were quick to take offence.

At 16, Nicole went to Melbourne to work. But she started going out with a local footballer and eventually moved back to Shepparton and a job in a local business. In early 2000, she met Ken Mansell, by then retired from the force. She asked him what he knew about her mother's death.

He told her things she had been too young to realise back in 1991: that her father had started the affair before her mother's death and had been short of money. He said he had saved the inquest brief in case it was ever reinvestigated.

Nicole told her brothers what Mansell had said and confronted her father. 'He denied it all, but when I asked why we have never talked about Mum's death he broke down.'

King's hold over his children was slipping. In early 2004, Nicole and her husband moved to Adelaide, and Peter moved to Sydney near Jason. John was still at Stanhope but had left the old shop he had shared with his father.

In February this year, Jason asked his brothers and Nicole to his apartment in Sydney to discuss their mother's death. It was the first time they had all talked about it together, calm and sober. Jason told them he had been doing some digging and had found some unsettling facts – including one about a life insurance policy. He said he was going to the police.

GRAEME Robert King's world has shrunk to a dingy back room behind a long-dead shop in the quiet main street of Stanhope, a sleepy town on the edge of the Goulburn Valley.

King has dark eyes, swarthy skin, a Zapata moustache, crew-cut greying hair, a loud voice and the manner of a man used to getting his own way. His own way is living alone on WorkCover payments and drinking at Stanhope Bowls Club.

Some who know him are nervous of the man he was rather than the one he is. At 54, the effects of time, alcohol, tobacco, a bachelor diet and old injuries have slowed him. He limps, and one big hand hangs askew below a stiff shoulder, though there are still signs of the athlete he was in the powerful shoulders and arms.

He sits, as worn as the ancient Staffordshire terrier at his feet – though not as happy as she is – and chain smokes Longbeach cigarettes from a giant economy pack. After an hour of football, farms and cows he finally allows the conversation to be steered to his wife and how she died.

His foot jiggles furiously. He warns he is taping the conversation because he knows what people say: that if his wife didn't die accidentally, he killed her. 'Hell, yeah,' he exclaims when asked if he is aware that people suspect him. He confronted someone recently after hearing they were spreading gossip about him. But he insists he didn't move from Katandra to get away from the stares and whispers of people who knew him and liked Kaye.

He tells the story he told the police fourteen years ago. Now, as then, he remembers some details clearly but not others. He says shock played havoc with his memory. This could explain why he paints a rosy picture of his last hours with a woman who was, on the evidence of friends and family, planning to leave him.

He says they went to bed after milking the cows that morning – 'we made love' – then watched a Nicole Kidman film he says Kaye taped the night before, when he was out at a meeting. He says they had lunch together before he went to fetch the boys from the neighbour's house. Meanwhile, he claims, Kaye would get in those cows that hadn't been milked earlier.

He says he 'had a yarn' with the neighbour then drove home via the Katandra shop. As they got home, he says, he saw the cattle milling around the haystack. He recalls sending the boys looking for Kaye, then pulling her out of the pit – 'a hell of a job' – but it's all a blur after that. The shock, he explains helpfully. He started smoking again that day and hasn't stopped since.

On the dusty walls are old show sashes, fading photographs of long-dead champion cows, a copy of Jesaulenko's mark of the century, a North Melbourne jumper signed by Wayne Carey.

In the corner, over the fireplace, is an old picture frame. Stuck in it is a photograph of him and Kaye on their wedding day: two handsome country kids, standing under a tree in a churchyard, gazing into the future as innocently as every young couple does. Smoke has dulled the glass and the photograph is losing its lustre.

Would he ever get married again? Tried to a couple of times, he grunts, but it didn't happen. You get used to living alone, he adds.

Besides, he says softly, I'll never get another one like Kaye. And he lights another cigarette.

ALTHOUGH the autopsy report stated that the cause of Kaye King's death was unascertainable, it was quickly accepted as a freak accident, except by some close family members and their friends. At the time of publication, police from the homicide squad's 'cold case' unit are investigating.

6.
BLUE MAGIC

RACETRACKS are full of shrewd people but few prudent ones. A more cautious man than John Seaton might have sensed the danger sooner, but Seaton was a gambler – a high roller who bet big on the turn of a card and lavished millions on harness horses. In business, he once bought a mob of 35,000 sheep knowing he would lose a fortune if the market wavered. It didn't, and another Seaton deal became lore. Big John had *mana*, the Maori word that fits prestige, ego, potency and confidence into four letters. When he made his last telephone call on November 14, 2004 – the last night of his life – he seemed characteristically cocky, as defiant of public opinion and police inquiries as 30 million self-made dollars can make a big operator in a small place like Christchurch, prim and mostly proper capital of New Zealand's pastoral South Island.

Earlier that evening, as usual, Seaton had called a stock agent to discuss buying sheep at the coming week's sales. He'd also talked to his solicitor, as he did on Sunday nights. Now it was late and he was talking to a mate, Mick Guerin.

Guerin is racing editor of *The New Zealand Herald* and Seaton was one of the biggest harness racing owners he'd known in decades of covering the gallops and harness racing. But this time the call was more personal than professional. Guerin wasn't fishing for a story.

There was a kind heart underneath his hard-bitten racetrack persona.

He was wondering how Seaton was handling two problems that had ambushed him in previous months – one intensely personal, the other painfully public.

Seaton had grown used to being in control, but these twin troubles were outside his control. First, his wife Ann had relapsed with a grave illness that had been in remission. The second problem was the devastating charge that he had conspired in racehorse doping. Specifically, that he had connived with his high-profile harness trainer, Mark Purdon, to treat one of his top horses with an allegedly performance-enhancing drug dubbed 'blue magic'.

Seaton had vehemently denied the allegation and wasn't about to back down. Agitated about media coverage of the case, he had demanded an apology from a prominent Christchurch newspaper which implied he had wanted to boost the horse's race record in order to sell it at a higher price, an accusation which, if proved, would leave him open to criminal fraud charges.

Seaton had then inflamed the situation by abusing harness-racing officials at the New Zealand Trotting Cup meeting at Addington Raceway on November 12, 2004. He accused them of deliberately humiliating him by making the charges public in the peak week of New Zealand's harness racing and social calendar.

In one outburst, the millionaire called Harness Racing New Zealand's chief executive, Edward Rennell, 'a low prick', clenching his fist and threatening to 'deal' with him. In another ugly and embarrassing scene, he abused a racecourse detective and several harness-racing executives.

To Rennell it seemed 'irrational', a glimpse of inner turmoil. The quietly-spoken Rennell was shocked by the incident but did not feel that he had to apologise for doing his job, which was to keep harness-racing clean. A tough gig, some cynics would suggest.

Talking to Guerin on the telephone two nights after his outbursts, Seaton seemed calmer – but still determined to clear his name and take on his perceived enemies. Seaton told Guerin the same thing he had already told others that weekend: that he and Purdon were innocent and that he'd fight the charges to the end.

No-one doubted he would have a red hot go. He had the deepest pockets south of Wellington to fund his defence, and had already retained a Queen's Counsel known for taking no prisoners in court. When it came to confrontation, Seaton took his cue from the All Blacks.

At 55, Seaton looked bold and bluff and bulletproof. Ruthless in business but generous when he won, he loved being the life of the party. He was, in Australian terms, a backblocks John Singleton with a larrikin edge that didn't quite suit polite South Island society, which retained something of the reserve that had come across from Britain with the first white settlers.

Seaton's considerable fortune was built on his own nerve and judgment. His rise from semi-literate farm boy to truck driver to sheep dealer and property and racing tycoon is legendary on the agricultural South Island, where every other farmer breeds or races a harness horse. The lush farmland of the Canterbury Plain west of Christchurch is a Monopoly board of English place names, and John Seaton was the biggest player in the game in those parts.

Or he was until early on November 15, 2004. Some time around dawn that Monday, as the wind moaned through the hedges and windbreaks of his showpiece property at Aylesbury, and the hounds of the Christchurch Hunt bayed mournfully in their kennels next door, Seaton's private demons broke through the facade he displayed to the world.

He took a gun into the bathroom of the big farmhouse and shot himself.

He wasn't bulletproof after all.

CLOSE to 2000 mourners gathered at the big man's funeral – too many for a church, so the service was held at the Christchurch Convention Centre, not far from Addington Raceway, trotting's spiritual home in Australasia and scene of Seaton's greatest triumphs as an owner.

It was there that the best of the scores of horses he raced, Il Vicolo, won the New Zealand Derby in 1994 and two New Zealand Cups in 1995 and 1996 (recouping in stakes more than $1.5 million of the many millions he'd spent on the sport).

It was the biggest harness-racing funeral in New Zealand or Australia since the death – also by self-inflicted gunshot – of another popular larrikin, the champion reinsman Vinnie Knight, in Victoria in 1991.

But a strange thing struck mourners: although racing people had come from all over New Zealand and Australia to be there, racing and horses were not once mentioned in the service. It was like sending off Sinatra without mentioning singing. Hundreds of people who had known Seaton only from the racetrack, stud and sales ring listened in astonishment to a lopsided eulogy that referred only to his other life as a sheep dealer and farmer.

It must have been unnerving for his trainer, close friend and co-accused, Mark Purdon, a member of New Zealand's most famous trotting family. It seemed clear that Seaton's ailing widow, Ann, and their daughter, Ann-Marie, blamed harness-racing officials – and perhaps even the sports itself – for his death.

The muttered accusation was that a jealous industry influenced by the steely Christchurch establishment had deliberately lopped a tall poppy for a minor misdemeanour.

There was, perhaps, another and darker interpretation to be made: that Seaton's name was so tarnished by the doping scandal that his mortified family and friends were pretending it had never happened.

But no amount of wishful thinking could stop the gossip. People asked why a man worth $A30million would kill himself. Some speculated that there must be more to it. The 'blue magic' saga was certainly tragic – but was it also sinister?

CONSPIRACY theorists had plenty to work with. Seaton's sudden death was not the first connected to the case. Four months earlier, the man at the centre of the doping investigation had also killed himself. His name was Robert Asquith. He had returned to New Zealand only a few months before his death, and was the Australian connection in a racket that unsettled racing on both sides of the Tasman.

Asquith had some things in common with John Seaton, though $30 million wasn't one of them. He was tall, good-looking and extroverted, and liked racing, gambling and big-noting. A friend of Asquith's said of the pair: 'One had money; the other wanted money'.

Seaton knew Asquith had 'blue magic', which meant each had something the other could use. Security footage studied by police showed that Asquith and Seaton had rubbed shoulders in Club Aspinall, the high rollers' room at the Christchurch Casino. Whereas Seaton could afford to lose $10,000 a night, Asquith merely pretended he could.

Behind Asquith's confident front, his life had run off the rails. There were rumours of an affair with a younger woman, the sort of escapade that had led him to leave New Zealand suddenly in the late 1990s, followed by his long-suffering wife, Jill.

Then, at 47, he had been charged by New Zealand police under the Medicines Act with possession of a drug he used for horse doping. Technically, it was a minor offence and probably would have meant only a fine, but the real stakes were higher. The charge followed months of pressure as the scam unravelled, exposing him as a fraud and a failure – and as a potential informer against anyone he had supplied with 'blue magic'.

On July 20, 2004, two days before Asquith was due in court, his wife found a note in the neat brick house on their pleasant farmlet near Oxford, a sleepy town tucked below picture postcard snow-capped alps an hour's drive north-west of Christchurch. She called the police. They found Asquith's body hanging in an outbuilding.

The answers to questions that stewards and police wanted to ask had died with Asquith. He was the only person who knew the facts behind the 'blue magic' story – such as who had been using the drug, and who had the inside knowledge to back the horses injected with it. Whether Rob Asquith would have told the complete truth, of course, was debatable. He was careless with facts. Still, some people in harness and thoroughbred racing in both countries might have felt a twinge of relief when they heard he was dead. After all, who knows what he might have said under pressure?

As racing scandals go, the 'blue magic' affair did not seem as dramatic or outrageous as when the galloper Rocket Racer won the 1987 Perth Cup by nine lengths on 'elephant juice' before collapsing in distress and later dying. And there was no Fine Cotton moment – as at Brisbane's Eagle Farm in 1984 – when outraged punters jeered 'ring-in' and 'wrong horse' at the horse's nervous handlers, who did not fear the authorities as much as the ruthless but stupidly reckless Sydney betting men who'd ordered the switch and then highlighted the shambolic rort by leaking the information and plunging huge bets on it all over Australia, Papua New Guinea and in the Pacific islands.

The few people who know exactly when the drug they called 'the blue' was first used in Victoria are quiet about it. But by late 2003, there were whispers of a drug in harness racing that was going undetected by routine swabbing.

It was said that some trainers around Mildura in the far north-west of the state were giving horses more than bran mashes. How long it had been going on was unclear. A couple of extra wins in a season might not attract attention, but a couple is rarely enough.

A winning edge is hard to refuse and even harder to hide. Statistics eventually tell the story, even if rival trainers, owners and drivers don't. When a pattern emerges showing a big improvement in horses prepared by particular trainers, suspicions harden. In this case, perhaps, the first win to raise eyebrows was in a race at Victoria's city track, Moonee Valley, on October 31, 2003.

At the advanced age of twelve years (horses usually die of old age in their twenties), a brown gelding with the unlikely name of Our Equal Opportunity had hardly set the harness world on fire. In fact, he had never won at a city meeting in 142 starts. His form suggested he never would. But he did win that night, a 'first-up' victory after what was apparently a long and beneficial spell away from racing.

Punters might have wondered if Our Equal Opportunity had been spelled at Lourdes, not Ballarat, so miraculous was the improvement. But it's likely the form reversal was due to more prosaic reasons.

The old horse's new trainer was a Ballarat horseman called Rod Weightman, who had trained him for only a few weeks. Weightman, then 37, had not had many horses, but over the previous decade had gradually built up his annual tally of starters from a handful to more than 50. The son of a seasoned harness man, he'd inherited his father's touch in patching up old campaigners to coax a few good runs out of them. In the ten seasons ending August 31, 2003, Weightman's annual strike rate of winners to starters rose from zero (admittedly from only nine starters) in 1993–94 to a high of 35 per cent (six wins from seventeen starters) in 1997–98, to average twenty per cent overall, a figure that only the most astute trainers achieve.

There was no doubt Weightman could train winners. The trouble was, he started to train too many. In the 2002–03 season, he averaged a believable 23 per cent strike rate with fifteen winners from 63 starts. But in the new season, starting September 2003, he ran red-hot, as the saying goes.

By the time the posse caught up with him eight months later, he had trained 31 winners from 69 starts – a stunning strike rate of 45 per cent. And he was doing it with cheap old horses that had lost their early form, bought out of 'claiming races' for a few thousand dollars each. They weren't winning much before he got them, less after he got rid of them.

Take Weightman's favourite, 'a magnificent old fella' that rejoiced in the name Angus Puddleduck, who had lost form while trained for his original owners. Weightman knew he could make 'the Duck' fly. He got him on Boxing Day, 2003. A month later, he won at Maryborough, the first of four straight wins.

Early in March 2004, Ballarat police began surveillance of people suspected of handling drugs and stolen property. Among the properties under watch was one belonging to Rod Weightman.

One of the police on the case had once worked for the racing squad. He suggested that as Weightman was a licensed trainer, Harness Racing Victoria stewards might just happen to fancy being on hand when his property was searched.

The stewards jumped at the opportunity to accept this thoughtful offer.

So it was that on a cold, foggy morning on April 28, police with guns and dogs raided Weightman's property as similar teams swooped on five other houses around the district. The phlegmatic Weightman didn't make a fuss. He is not that sort. But when they led him, handcuffed, into the backyard, he saw the stewards waiting for him and muttered, 'That really tops off the morning'.

Something told him they wanted to talk about the 62 unlabelled vials of blue liquid the police had found in his refrigerator. Compared with that, the stolen ride-on mower and a bag of cannabis in one of the sheds were the least of his problems.

Two days later, Harness Racing Victoria suspended Weightman indefinitely, pending analysis of the blue liquid and a full inquiry. He was also bailed on various criminal charges, for which he would eventually be fined a total of $4400. Weightman ducked questions about what the blue liquid was or where he obtained it, but the stewards already had a fair idea.

A reliable source had slipped them a sample of 'the blue' a few weeks earlier and even before the laboratory tests were done, they were confident the 62 vials held the same prohibited drug – propantheline bromide.

It had been supplied by Robert Asquith, late of Ballarat via Queensland, who had recently returned to New Zealand's greener fields where he had been so busy hawking his blue mixture that, in the same week the Australian authorities made their move, the Christchurch police and racing stewards already had him – and the people he'd been dealing with – in their sights.

For a man who said he was related to Herbert Asquith, the puritanical British prime minister who became the first Earl of Oxford, Robert Asquith had some bad habits. He chain-smoked and drank so much coffee he would have tested positive to caffeine if the stewards had swabbed him as carefully as the horses he backed.

As a gambler, he wasn't only a punter: he played baccarat in casinos and boasted he could 'beat the house' at blackjack, a claim that was unlikely to be true. There was no doubt he was both clever and a con man, a Walter Mitty-type figure with delusions that led him to dream up oddball get-rich-quick schemes.

One such scheme was to fleece suckers by advertising a sure-fire 'cure' for shortness – the plan being to mail anyone who sent money an old telephone book they could stand on to measure themselves. He set up a male escort agency to provide escorts for older wealthy women. He invented a plastic meal tray he hoped to sell to McDonald's (they didn't buy it), and he designed a line of 'comical' greeting cards that no-one else thought funny.

When Asquith and his wife turned up at Ballarat some time in 1999, they didn't look like a success story. They were driving an old car and looking for somewhere cheap to live in Miners Rest, a horse-training district next to Dowling Forest racecourse.

A retired policeman let them move into a converted loft above his stables 'for a year or two' in return for looking after his young horses. Asquith, a tall man in his early 40s, told his landlord they had been in Queensland since leaving New Zealand, though he said little about what they had done there. He gave the impression he had been a leading New Zealand reinsman and had driven horses 'in America and Canada'. This was an exaggeration: he had been an also-ran trotting trainer before handing in his licence in 1994 after being caught illegally importing hormonal drugs.

Jill Asquith, later described by a neighbour as a 'natural horsewoman who married badly', got a permit to train gallopers at Ballarat. It didn't go well.

In more than three seasons, she was to train just three winners from 54 starters. Then, in mid-2003, she was suspended and fined when one of her horses returned an illegally high bicarbonate reading. This was the result of a 'milkshake', a drench given to improve stamina by reducing lactic acid in tired muscles.

Robert Asquith, meanwhile, promoted himself as a horse chiropractor. As he got to know trainers who wanted horses manipulated, he offered to treat them with unprescribed drugs. The source was not explained, although some suspected the chemicals came from Mexico via Sydney and that Asquith mixed the solutions himself, using various food dyes to provide different colours before settling on blue. The name 'blue magic' was coined when the story was first broken by an alert racing writer called Adam Hamilton in the *Herald Sun*.

Asquith slipped from stable to stable. Some trainers gave him a wide berth – either on principle or because he made them nervous. Others would try anything that might give them an edge – provided it wasn't 'swabbable', as they say in racing to describe any substance not known to be detectable by conventional swabbing.

Asquith, as much con man as horseman, took a shrewd guess that Victorian authorities weren't yet testing specifically for propantheline, and confidently claimed his solution wasn't detectable.

He offered discounts if told which horses were to be treated, so he could punt on them. This also might have been shrewd salesmanship – at least in some cases. It was later discovered that not all the vials of blue liquid he sold contained propantheline; some had only the food dye that gave it the distinctive colour.

By accident or design, Asquith seemed to deal mostly with harness trainers – some of them at Mildura, hundreds of kilometres away from his home base at Ballarat, which is much less than two hours drive west of Melbourne. This connection with harness racing could have been because he had a natural rapport with harness racing people, who tend to favour chiropractic manipulation, massage and acupuncture to relieve spinal problems in their horses caused by the unnatural pacing gait.

There is also a faint suggestion that harness racing – seen as galloping's poor relation – had more 'desperate' and perhaps more gullible trainers, many of them small-time operators who combined training with other forms of income. It's possible some galloping people avoided Asquith and his bag of tricks because they were fully-fledged professionals who had big stables and far more to lose if anything went wrong.

There is an Australian racing adage: 'Never trust a Kiwi or an alsatian dog.' While such attitudes are patently unfair, probably racist and possibly illegal, they linger in some quarters. Racing people might be superstitious but they are also suspicious.

One leading Ballarat thoroughbred trainer, a robust character whose stables are near the entrance to Dowling Forest racetrack, told the author that Asquith approached him offering to 'help' his horses, but that he'd refused point blank.

The trainer said he didn't believe in chiropractors and wanted nothing to do with anything else Asquith might have been peddling.

As the trainer had already been disqualified for some time over allegedly 'tubing' his horses with 'milkshakes', he was entitled to be wary of any offers of artificial stimulants.

Racing people can be warm-hearted and generous but racecourse gossip is vicious – and often inaccurate. Gossip later linked the Ballarat trainer and at least two other successful galloping trainers with 'blue magic', but there is not even circumstantial evidence to support such a theory.

Each of the three trainers prepared plenty of winners before and after the 'blue-magic' scandal. Unlike Rod Weightman's, their strike rates did not appear to alter much either way.

Living in a glorified shed with a few slow racehorses away from family and friends must have worn down Jill Asquith, then in her late 30s.

The respectable butcher's daughter from Oamaru had married Asquith as a teenager, had two daughters by him (since grown, and living in England) and had stuck with him despite his various vices. Jill Asquith was homesick, but staying in

Australia gave her husband a greater chance to turn a quick dollar to fuel his gambling. He did make some money – though not enough for a house. They paid $90,000 for a few hectares with a hayshed near the racecourse and converted the shed into stables and a room to live in. It was a shrewd buy. The pity was that Asquith's preoccupation with making a dishonest dollar ultimately prevented them from turning an honest one when they had the chance.

The long-suffering Jill mixed cement while Robert laid it, and they toiled to build an elaborate front fence with concrete posts and painted rails to set the place off.

They lined the shed and converted it into stables with a flat upstairs but that was as far as it got. They picked out a house site elsewhere on the block but nothing came of it before their life all went wrong yet again.

Meanwhile, word spread and Asquith kept moving the mysterious blue stuff. It was at this stage, in late 2003, that Rod Weightman, who trained on the other side of Ballarat, asked Asquith to 'look at' his horses after hearing on the grapevine about other trainers gaining a winning edge, the most coveted thing in racing.

Weightman was soon willingly paying $150 a shot for 'the blue', although he insists it did not improve all horses and only marginally improved the others. Either way, there's little doubt most of the 31 winners he trained from September 2003 until his arrest in April the following year had been injected with the drug.

What saved Weightman from a suspension even longer than the five years and three months he is currently serving, was that only seven of the many urine samples held by the authorities came up positive when retested for propantheline after his arrest.

The man who cheerfully calls himself the scapegoat for the blue magic affair doesn't hold many grudges. For a start, he says, he is still alive. He is bemused that two men whose involvement was still unproven – and might have stayed that way – would kill themselves 'when I'm the one found with 62 vials of the stuff in my fridge'.

Weightman is a chunky, calm little man with a professional horseman's strong hands. His slow drawl and dry humour belie alert eyes, which dart around the Ballarat pub-TAB agency where he meets people these days. He likes to know who is coming in the door and which races are coming up on the television screen.

He is torn between the code of silence and wanting to tell the oldest and best story in racing – how we beat the bookies. Weightman claims to have no regrets – 'I needed the holiday' – but is proud enough of his considerable training ability to resent being written off as a cheat who couldn't win without drugs.

He cites his career record at improving old horses with skill and patience, and insists he wasn't using 'the blue' until late 2003.

The authorities stripped him of seven of his 31 wins after the new drug tests, but he's still living well on the proceeds of the rest. He sold his farm, horse truck and gear, and bought a house in town with a swimming pool and spa 'because I want to do a bit of entertaining', he quips.

Weightman says he backed his winners but bet only '$500 to a grand' and scoffs at suggestions of organised crime connections and big betting coups. 'Nothing that dramatic,' he says, and seems unworried enough to be genuine.

Ask him if the rest of the samples must have deteriorated and he shrugs, deadpan. Ask if swabs from other trainers' horses might also have deteriorated and he smiles. Ask if any thoroughbred racehorses were on the stuff and he laughs outright. Of course, he says.

When the story of Weightman's arrest broke last May, he did his own code of harness racing a backhanded favour by saying he had backed gallopers that had been treated with 'blue magic'.

When thoroughbred racing investigators asked for details, he lost his memory.

Later, it seemed he got some of it back. Weightman told the author that he knew of several gallopers that raced on propantheline. He cites an '80-1 shot at Flemington with three duck eggs beside its name that jumped out of the ground and ran a place. A good thing beaten'.

But he won't be telling any tales. 'Why would I want to name names?' he asks. 'What good would that do? I might get a bullet in the head.'

Then he stares at the television screen, distracted. He's backed a pacer at Cranbourne and, sure enough, it gets up. He still knows a winner when he sees one. It's in the blood. Even when 'blue magic' isn't.

SO what is 'blue magic'? The active ingredient of the solution is not blue and, according to some experts, not necessarily magic. Nor is it new.

Rumoured to have been used on harness horses in North America since the late 1980s, propantheline bromide was detected in Canada in 1994 and came to Australia soon afterwards, when it was reputedly known as 'Canadian pink'. Racing, like the drug sub-culture, has an unerring instinct for coining catchy names.

It was first detected in Australian racing at Sydney's Harold Park Raceway on September 12, 1997, when a leading reinsman, Jason Proctor, was disqualified for fifteen months after his horse, My Paleface Navajo, returned a positive swab. The suspension stalled what had seemed a brilliant career. Proctor, then 22, led both the Hunter Valley drivers' and trainers' premiership tables, had set new records in both premierships in the 1995–1996 season and was New South Wales' leading junior driver for the previous four seasons.

But after his suspension (on this and other drug charges), Proctor lost his winning edge. He now struggles to be in the top 25 NSW drivers and trainers.

Harness-racing insiders believe Proctor was not the only trainer to use prohibited drugs over several years, and that propantheline has also been used in thoroughbred racing.

The champion reinsman Brian Hancock, a staunch opponent of drug use, once endured more than 100 consecutive losses at Harold Park, a 'slump' some believe was due to a few rival trainers using a range of drugs that made some horses virtually unbeatable at their own level.

Hancock will not go on the record about his suspicions while he is still a licensed trainer and driver, but off the record he is a savage critic of drug cheats – and the way some of them have allegedly got away with wrongdoing for years.

Drug detection has certainly been patchy. In 1998, former world champion driver Ted Demmler – who knew John Seaton, coincidentally – was suspended for nine months when his horse Breenys Fella tested positive to propantheline, despite a strong case that his veterinarian legitimately administered the drug to settle the horse's stomach on the long trip from Victoria.

In May 2003, a New Zealand veterinarian found a vial of blue liquid at a harness-racing stable near Invercargill and sent it for analysis, but no action was taken.

In May 2004, a trainer called Doug Willis was prosecuted

when his horse Rocket Score tested positive to a 'bronchial dilator' similar to propantheline at Harold Park. Propantheline and its derivatives have been used in humans to treat stomach ulcers.

Its legitimate veterinary use is to relax the muscles of pregnant mares for rectal examinations. The 'blue magic' name derives from food dye added as a marketing device.

Similar solutions have reputedly been supplied in several colours.

Though there is not yet scientific proof that the drug enhances a racehorse's performance, authorities believe it can marginally lift stamina in stayers by dilating veins, airways and lungs to allow more efficient distribution of oxygen.

Racetrack wisdom has it that it is of little use to sprinters but is suited to Australasian harness racing, in which horses race over relatively long distances.

It is not a stimulant like caffeine or the notorious 'elephant juice' (etorphine), which boost heart rate and cause the animal to move abnormally fast. Instead, it helps the animal to maintain an existing speed for longer, in the way that altitude training might.

Anecdotally, propantheline is considered more effective in helping older horses regain lost form than helping young, healthy horses find winning form.

'It does not make slow horses fast,' says one well-informed trainer. 'If a horse is already fit and has enough ability, it makes a good thing into a certainty.'

However, harness-racing stewards believe the drug is usually sufficiently effective to change the pattern of racing, with horses winning regardless of how well or poorly they may be driven.

Edward Rennell, the chief steward in Christchurch abused by

John Seaton, is certain he has seen horses win despite being 'extravagantly' driven around fields in a way that would usually ensure a horse ran out of stamina before the line. He and his Australian counterparts in harness racing suggest that some drivers have driven far more conservatively since the drug was exposed.

Galloping stewards have not been so forthcoming. As far as the thoroughbred racing industry is concerned, 'blue magic' had nothing to do with them.

THE STORY SO FAR ...

April 28, 2004: 62 vials of blue liquid found at harness trainer Rod Weightman's house near Ballarat. Weightman stood down.

May 4: Six New Zealand racing stables raided. NZ analysts identify propantheline in samples obtained by an informer.

May 27: NZ police charge Robert Asquith with selling the drug.

June 1: First Victorian positive swab for propantheline.

June 3: NZ harness legend Mark Purdon charged with using the drug.

July 7: Seven Weightman swabs test positive.

July 21: Robert Asquith found dead at home in Oxford, New Zealand.

July 26: Weightman disqualified for 63 months on seven charges.

July 28: Mildura trainer Andrew Vozlic disqualified for twelve months for using propantheline on one horse and twelve months for elevated bicarbonate levels in three horses.

July 29: Trainers Martin Herbert and Clayton Tonkin disqualified for a year and fined heavily for using propantheline.

November 13: Prominent NZ owner John Seaton and his trainer Mark Purdon charged over alleged use of propantheline.

November 15: Seaton found dead at his luxury Canterbury Plain property.

> With big money comes big risks,
> which is why the industry has always
> tended to attract tough people ...

7.
THE ABALONE RANGERS

AT sunset a curious scene unfolds in a windswept paddock overlooking Bass Strait. A mob of black steers stare and snort at the strange thing that has suddenly appeared in their quiet world. You would think they had never seen a man dressing himself in camouflage gear before. Cattle have short memories – the visitor has been here often, and each time follows the same routine, watched by his four-legged audience.

Minutes earlier he planted his car nearby, behind a friendly farmer's shed. Now he's under a tree, hidden from the road, kitting himself out in pants, jacket, hat, leggings and hiking boots. Camouflaged and waterproof, the big man grabs his bag and heads across the paddock towards the shoreline.

Out of sight, somewhere to his right, one of his mates is already settled in, sweeping the landscape with binoculars, watching his back.

He climbs a fence, vaults another, then crosses rough country close to the cliff, avoiding the skyline. He hides, melting into the gorse and long grass, and sets up a mounted telescope and scans the horizon through it. He looks like a sniper stalking and staking out the enemy and, in a way, he is. His name is Rod Barber and he is one of a small army fighting a guerrilla war against thieves who raid the seas for shellfish so prized they have been hunted to near extinction almost everywhere but southern Australia.

Back at his desk, pecking at a keyboard in a bland government office in a seaside town, he is another public servant with the Fisheries division of Victoria's Department of Primary Industries. But out here – patrolling more than 200 kilometres of cliffs, beaches and bays on the Mornington Peninsula – he is the abalone ranger.

FOR an overgrown saltwater snail that can be as tough as tyre rubber, abalone has a big reputation and an even bigger price tag. In Asian cultures it is the cocaine of cuisine: from Tokyo to Hong Kong and in Chinatowns everywhere it is coveted for its distinctive taste and supposed aphrodisiac qualities, linked to the fact that the naked shellfish is traditionally seen as resembling female genitalia.

Until the 1960s the Asian taste for abalone barely registered in Australia, where so-called 'mutton fish' was dismissed as little better than bait. But as world abalone fisheries started to collapse, demand reached southern Australia. Fishermen and weekend divers started selling abalone to Chinese restaurants and a lucrative trade – both black market and legal – was born.

In one generation, the Australian abalone industry has become a multi-million dollar concern. In Tasmania and Victoria, the two strongest wild fisheries left in the world, it is the biggest fishing export earner of all. Along the way, it has made millionaires out of a relatively few people lucky enough to be in the right place at the right time – and bold and smart enough to grasp the opportunity.

The first Australian abalone licences were issued in the 1960s. In Victoria from 1962 to 1968, licence endorsements cost £3, or $6. In Tasmania the first two licence holders, who recall paying £10 each in 1965, still dive 40 years later. They are among 125 Tasmanian licensees who have seen their meagre investment turn into the equivalent of a lottery win. In a market based on a commodity that is as tightly controlled as De Beers diamonds, the price of a Victorian licence has jumped from $80,000 in 1981 to peak at roughly $7 million last year.

The abalone kings are rarely seen in the social pages but they could buy and sell some of those who are. One licence holder recently sold a huge house in one of Melbourne's premier streets for $6 million. In Victoria, the most exclusive brotherhood of wealthy white males is not the Melbourne Club or the stock exchange, but the 71 millionaires created by a licence system set up to protect abalone stocks but which, in effect, also protects licensees. Not that it makes the task of diving for the shellfish any easier or safer.

With big money comes big risks, which is why the industry has always tended to attract tough people, some of them willing to bend or break the law. Australia's biggest known amphetamine producer, John William Samuel Higgs, who has been jailed for manslaughter and drug trafficking, owned a seafood plant and a trawler that police suspect were fronts for illegal abalone processing. A man who owed Higgs money drowned in sinister circumstances in 1992.

When a Victorian undercover policeman, Lachlan McCulloch, arrested a heavy drug trafficker called Peter Pilarinos in the 1990s, he was astonished when Pilarinos asked him to invest $200,000 in illegal abalone to sell to Melbourne's Chinatown restaurants.

'He promised to double the money in a month,' McCulloch

says. He has little doubt the offer was genuine. Naturally, he refused, but being a keen recreational diver and fisherman, he was intrigued by the abalone scene.

Eating abalone might be healthy; supplying it often isn't. The greatest hazard facing divers deep underwater is not sharks but the bends – the ill-effects of nitrogen bubbles in the bloodstream caused by diving too deep, too long and coming up too fast. Few of the early divers who ignored warnings about deep diving are now alive. Others have crumbling bones, ruined joints and addled brains.

Small boats and rough seas are also deadly. Victorian Fisheries officers know of at least three suspected poachers who have drowned in recent years. One poacher reputedly lost three deckhands in separate incidents, and is now so deeply affected by the tragedies – and the effects of diving and drugs – that he lives like a hermit in hidden bush camps on crown land. Serial poacher Cam Strachan once brought home the body of a diver who died of a brain haemorrhage in Bass Strait. Fearing he would be accused of manslaughter if police pulled him over, Strachan left the body in the boat as he towed it from Port Welshpool (on Victoria's east coast) to a country hospital. 'It was a horror show,' Strachan recalls. 'As rigor mortis set in, his arm raised up and stuck out of the boat as we drove along the highway.'

Poachers stand to lose cars, boats, equipment and their liberty. They risk their lives because they take chances with bad weather, rough coastline and dark nights to dodge detection. One night, near where Rod Barber was recently staked out on the Mornington Peninsula, two wannabe poachers speeding back to Port Phillip Bay with no lights slammed their expensive Shark Cat into a rock called Pope's Eye. One of them fractured his spine. He was lucky. People die poaching.

With Barber, it's not a case of poacher turned gamekeeper, but he knows his enemy. Tall, strong and dangerously fit, he has been a diver since his teenage years and he understands the way poachers think and knows the risks they face. He watches the wind, tides and weather forecast the way the poachers do, and when the conditions are right – wind offshore, light swell, good visibility – he and his colleagues go out and watch and wait. Sometimes, if they have a tip-off, it's for days at a time, crouching in hides with sandwiches and water bottles.

They joke about themselves being 'fish pigs' but at the sharp end their job is no laughing matter. Few junior police officers, for instance, would regularly pursue lawbreakers with so much to lose – or gain.

As in police crime squads, there is a competitive camaraderie among the Fisheries officers that encourages them to go the extra mile in an effort to beat the villains. Which is why, at Easter and long weekends – the times most people spend holidaying with family and friends – the keenest Fisheries officers often roster themselves on to work because it's also a good time for part-time poachers to hit the coast.

It is a cat-and-mouse routine. Barber and his colleagues take up positions in hides above the shoreline, connected by radios and powerful binoculars. They watch the swell lapping below them for signs of a shore-based diver at work. They sweep the windswept paddocks behind them, trying to spot the lookouts that poachers also post. Surveillance breeds counter-surveillance. As in war, it is long hours of boredom punctuated with furious action. And it has its dangers, on both sides. The cruel sea ensures that. An added degree of risk for all concerned is that poachers tend to work under cover of darkness or in weather conditions or in places where few recreational divers would go.

In February 2005 Barber was awarded an Australian Bravery Medal for swimming through high seas in the dark to rescue an injured abalone poacher trapped on the rocks. A week after the medal presentation, Barber's crew arrested another poacher on the same stretch of Victorian coast. A routine police check showed the man had just served eighteen years for murder. For Barber and his officers, who work unarmed, it was a reminder that the abalone business can be dangerous on both sides of the law. For a few, there is fast money – but there is never easy money.

ART imitates life, and so does Bryce Courtenay. No-one knows the value of true stories better than Australia's most prolific producer of popular fiction. When he based his latest blockbuster, *Brother Fish*, on a Bass Strait fisherman, one of many people his researchers turned to for advice was Mike Munday, a colourful Tasmanian abalone diver turned poacher turned lawyer. Munday's brief was to write about surviving the killer storms that make Bass Strait one of the most hazardous stretches of water in the world. He did it so well that Courtenay noted his help in *Brother Fish* and named a character after him.

Munday's 'perfect storm' scene stands out in the book. Such experiences are part of a remarkable life. Put in an orphanage at three when his parents separated, he was taken to Fiji at ten, where he learned to dive on coral reefs. At fourteen he was in a Salesian seminary in Melbourne, training to be a priest. At sixteen he returned to Tasmania. He was a bank teller in 1966 when his big brother Terry started taking abalone at weekends, duck-diving from a tractor tube.

Mike joined him. 'There were millions of abalone,' he recalls. 'We were only getting ten cents a pound but we could still make $100 in a day. I was getting $58 a week at the bank at the time.'

Later, when he worked night shift in a printing works to support university studies, he persuaded an older workmate it was worth bankrolling an abalone diving venture. 'I took him down to Eaglehawk Neck and filled a spud bag with 120 pounds of abs in fifteen minutes.' It was 24 times their pay rate on night shift. The investor bought a boat and a Land Rover to tow it; Munday and his brother each paid a few dollars for an abalone licence and went diving. He was eighteen.

The water was always cold and often dangerous – there was always the threat of running into a shark, stingray, octopus or killer whale – but it seemed to a bold youngster like picking up banknotes from the seabed. By the time he was 21, Munday was driving an E-type Jaguar and living in a waterfront apartment. He cut a figure that attracted equal parts admiration and jealousy. Success earns enemies.

'Cops would pull up beside me in the E-type and call me a drug dealer.' Some Fisheries officers of that era also resented younger men making big money, he claims. That he had been to university, was not a local fisherman's son and was willing to argue earned him some lasting grudges.

By the early 1970s, abalone prices had already begun to rocket. On one outing Munday pulled up about 1900 kilograms of shellfish. At more than $1 a kilo, it was a year's wages for a bank teller. But there were risks. His first brush with death came in 1971, when he was diving with Geoff Valentine, a big man who was to become a well-known stalwart in the industry.

Like Munday, Valentine had quit a religious vocation, leaving a monastery because he was more interested in cars and girls than a monk should be. On his first day diving, Valentine made more money than his father earned in a week. He soon had a new Ford Customline and a girlfriend. By the time he and Munday started diving together, he had married and fathered the first of seven children.

Tasmania's wild west coast was no place for outboard-powered runabouts – as opposed to trawler-sized 'mother ships' – but the pair risked it for the rich rewards of the abalone fields below the troubled waters. They loaded the runabout with two tonnes of the shellfish and were returning to the port of Strahan in the late afternoon. They didn't realise they were over a reef until a huge breaker exploded on it, smashing the boat and rolling them deep underwater. They thought they would die. Valentine was underwater for more than a minute, Munday even longer. The boat was in tiny pieces but the men had their wetsuits on, which probably saved their lives. Munday found first his flippers, then the boat's padded seat, floating in the debris. Both finds were minor miracles but they still needed a big miracle.

They were faced with a dreadful moral dilemma. Should they stick together and risk dying together – or was it each man for himself? Munday knew in his heart that the powerful Valentine had a good chance of saving himself but might perish trying to save his little mate. To his eternal gratitude the big man didn't hesitate and vowed to stick with him. The pair hung onto the floating boat seat and kicked, even 'surfing' down big waves. They were in their early 20s.

Had they been younger and more rash they might have headed straight for shore and died on the breakers on the reefs. Instead, they took the long route sideways towards the Cape Sorell lighthouse, blinking in the distance. By the time they crawled ashore, cold and exhausted, Valentine's nineteen-year-old wife, waiting back at Strahan with her baby, thought they were dead. At 3am a policeman knocked on her door to say her husband and his exhausted mate had staggered into the lighthouse up the coast.

Afterwards, Munday and Valentine went different ways. In 1972, Munday was working from a big boat with other divers when a cruiser called the *Janthe* sailed into Hobart and changed his life. At the helm was a man whose reputation preceded him. David Bryan Frith Strachan was then a rakish figure in his early 50s. A fighter pilot in World War II, he had flown airliners for TAA in the 1950s and '60s. A skilled sailor with no respect for authority, he passed on his skill, daring and cavalier attitude to his two sons, who were at school at Melbourne Grammar, one of Australia's finest and oldest private schools. By 1971 David

Strachan was diving for abalone in Bass Strait from his nineteen-metre 'gin palace'. Operating without a licence didn't faze him, but when he decided to try his luck on Tasmania's sheltered east coast he found the natives a little restless.

The *Hobart Mercury* newspaper noted the arrival of the 'luxurious cruiser *Janthe*' in February 1972. A reporter with a sharp eye for local pride and prejudice wrote that he found David Strachan 'lounging in a chair with his feet on a stool and a glass of scotch in his hand'. Strachan politely denied plotting an onslaught on the local abalone industry, but local divers weren't convinced. They elected the educated and articulate Mike Munday to confront the polished interloper with the message, 'We don't care where you poach, as long as it's not here'. Munday boarded the *Janthe* heart in mouth, expecting to be thrown into the harbour by what he imagined would be a crew of Melbourne villains. Instead, Strachan greeted him with a Johnny Walker at the bar and Sinatra on the stereo and talked of flying Beaufighters against the Japanese. He could have been that great Tasmanian Errol Flynn. Munday was captivated. He swapped sides: as a licensed Tasmanian abalone diver, he agreed to dive for the Victorian from the *Janthe*.

Munday's decision would ultimately cost him his ticket in the lucrative new industry. The authorities banned Strachan from sailing on his own boat after catching him diving, unlicensed, for abalone. When Munday helped sidestep this by taking over as skipper of the boat and paying Strachan a percentage of the catch, his cards were marked. One day in 1974 a Fisheries officer boarded the boat and measured more than 4000 abalone. In two nets in which the shellfish had not yet been checked, he found some that were slightly undersized – or, at least, that's the way Munday remembers it, and it hasn't been contradicted. The offence might seem trivial but it was enough to cost Munday his licence. In a stroke of a public service pen, Munday went from authorised diver to 'predatory' poacher, and stayed that way for

30 years. Ironically, he took far fewer abalone as a poacher than he would have been able to with a licence. (He saw licensed divers and unscrupulous processors collude to process vast numbers of 'over-quota' and sometimes undersized abalone.)

Along the way Munday enrolled in law school so he could defend himself. What he didn't know then was that David Strachan's older son would become a bigger Bass Strait poacher than Strachan senior had ever been. In fact, Munday's finest hour as a bush lawyer came when he got young Strachan out of jail with an appeal to the Supreme Court.

LIKE most schools, Melbourne Grammar has produced its mavericks. Two stand out. One now divides his life between London, Switzerland and New York and often appears in public and on television wearing women's clothes and thick make-up. His name is Barry Humphries. The other is – or was – the best-known abalone poacher in Australia, maybe the world. He is David Campbell Strachan, known as Cam. When he quit school at sixteen to work with his hands, he was the envy of more conventional classmates – many of them condemned to become mere leaders of industry, politics and the professions.

The entertainer and the abalone diver have little in common except perhaps a benign contempt for the old school tie and a manic edge that age has softened in Humphries but is still obvious in the younger man. Strachan admits to an obsessive-compulsive personality. He buzzes with nervous energy, fidgets like a kid on red cordial, and has tunnel vision – turning the high beam of a sharp practical intelligence on whatever has his attention, ignoring all else. Now, at 53, he is facing the fact that his past may ruin what is left of his life. The Grammar boy who made bad has a big reputation to live down if he is ever to get back on the water. Bail conditions on charges he is currently fighting ban him from being within one kilometre of the sea, except to work in one Westernport Bay boatshed.

Fisheries officers, police, prosecutors and magistrates have painted Strachan as the Black Prince of the illegal abalone market. In court, in headlines and news bulletins, he has been labelled a pirate, a thief and 'king of poachers'. The exhibitionist part of Strachan's character revels in this but he knows that his reputation has caused him more grief than pleasure or profit. He has made untold amounts of 'black money' but, as so often happens with unlawful enterprises and gamblers, he has lost all or most of it feeding his appetite for risk.

Even Strachan's opponents admire his ability as diver and seaman. Some have a soft spot for his larrikin style. In the boatshed where he works is a blown-up photograph of him driving a fast boat pursued by a police helicopter. It's like a scene from a Bond movie. On the back of the photograph is scrawled a chirpy message from particular Victorian Fisheries officers who have enjoyed hunting him for years. They are the best of enemies.

But Rod Barber says that the flip side of the Strachan legend is that for all his skill as a diver, seaman and boat builder, he is a failure as a criminal 'because given the years he's been in the game, he hasn't got a lot to show for it. He's been caught a hell of a lot'. Barber also points out that although Strachan correctly argues he has done much of his poaching around distant Bass Strait islands not usually harvested by licensed divers, he has caused long-term and ongoing damage to the fishery in both states by teaching a younger generation of divers how to poach. Although some – especially the man himself – might see Strachan as a Bass Strait 'bushranger' – part Robin Hood and part pied piper – to the authorities he is an opportunistic predator.

For all his acknowledged skill on and below the water, over 34 years Strachan has had more than 100 convictions, paid more than a million dollars in fines and still owes about $800,000, mostly in Tasmania. In the 1970s and 1980s, he would plead guilty and then go diving to pay for it. But asset seizure, massively increased fines and the threat of long jail sentences have scuppered his poaching career.

Strachan has had 'about twenty' boats confiscated. He has lost his own house and two belonging to his 85-year-old mother, all in blue-chip Brighton, one of Melbourne's most sought-after bayside suburbs. At the time of writing he rents a pleasant but small house in a modest outer suburb, drives a battered van and, when not in custody, works seven days a week building boats for game fishermen who fancy owning a Cam Strachan special. It's hard to believe that anyone who didn't have to, would work such punishing hours among fibreglass and polyester fumes.

'They've made it too tough. I can't do five years jail, and that's what I'm facing if I get caught again because poaching is now an indictable offence,' Strachan says. He always poached by boat rather than from the shore, but 'all the technology and modern communications mean you just can't do it any more. There's always someone with binoculars and a satellite telephone watching you.'

For a man who has smiled and cracked jokes while handcuffed, during high-speed chases and after being arrested at gunpoint by police, he is uncharacteristically sombre. Convicted of offering 690 kilos of black-market abalone to an undercover officer in 2003, he has been on bail since then pending an appeal. If the appeal fails, he faces up to eighteen months jail.

He has been jailed before – four times, in Tasmania and Victoria – but in mid-2005 he had two new reasons to stay out of trouble. Strachan's long-time partner, Samantha Seale, gave birth to twins, the result of prolonged treatment through an IVF program. His baby son and daughter mean a new start for Strachan. There is also a tragic echo in their arrival: a son and daughter borne by his first wife were killed in a car crash in

1984. His surviving daughter, now an adult, has a life-threatening illness. Some who know Strachan say the tragedy sent him into a frenzy of self-destructive behaviour from which he is still recovering. He was a man who didn't care. Now, he says, he does care.

There are other big abalone poachers – and many small ones – but Strachan always drew the most publicity. Where more discreet operators bent or broke the rules quietly, he flouted them. Where they mouthed apologies or feigned remorse, he was defiant and flippant. He built high-powered boats and drove them fearlessly through dangerous waters to outrun the law. He has crossed Bass Strait's notoriously treacherous waters hundreds of times. From Eden to Hobart, fishing and yachting people talk about Cam's exploits. He has the rare distinction of being known by his first name – even by virtual strangers who know him only by reputation.

He has been pursued often but the 'Big Chase' was in March 1998 when a fixed-wing aircraft, a police helicopter, five boats and 22 officers followed him across Bass Strait and along the Victorian coast for more than fourteen hours. A veteran Tasmanian marine police officer admitted grudgingly that it was the most outstanding display of boat handling he had seen.

Strachan tells stories – and produces photographs – of ferrying abalone from isolated Bass Strait islands by helicopter. On one poaching trip, he and a pilot (who later worked in war zones) crash-landed a light plane on a rough island airstrip, knocking off the wing tips when a mob of suicidal wallabies jumped into their path. Within two weeks he had conjured up a purpose-built catamaran to salvage the crippled aircraft and ship it to Victoria for rebuilding. It is still flying somewhere interstate.

Such exploits have made him a poster boy for poachers – and a whipping boy for the authorities. Which is understandable but not necessarily fair, says his friend Mike Munday, who sees desperation behind the bravado. 'Cam said to me after his kids were killed, "I've got nothing to lose." But now he has got something to lose.'

Munday argues that Strachan has provided a convenient scapegoat, targeted in Tasmania despite taking far less than the 'over quota' abalone that some licensed divers secretly sold through the back door to unscrupulous processors involved in both the black market and the legitimate market.

An example: Strachan made headlines in 1997 when caught with a few hundred abalone, at the same time that a well-known licensed diver barely raised a ripple when convicted by a Tasmanian magistrate of landing 9275 abalone 'without documentation'.

Munday says because Strachan's father was disliked in Tasmania, 'it's a case of the sins of the father being visited on the son'. But he stresses that his friend is now right out of chances. 'I've told him that if he gets caught again in Tasmanian waters – don't call me. I don't consider I've got a right to continue poaching because of the public money wasted trying to prosecute me. They spent maybe a million dollars of taxpayers' money chasing me around for three years with a net result that they lost when I took them to the Supreme Court in 2004 and proved the legislation was faulty. If it's good enough for me to give up, it's good enough for Cam.'

Strachan claims that since the early 1980s he has almost exclusively confined his 'fishing' to remote Bass Strait islands too distant and too difficult for Tasmanian divers, who get easier abalone closer to home. He circles a speck on the map called Albatross Island, off north-west Tasmania, and says that is where he has done most 'work'. The prevailing westerly winds there prevent diving most days, he says, and abalone-bearing 'rock bottom' runs out into deep water, kilometres from land, ensuring that millions of abalone stay safely out of reach forever. Strachan reckons Tasmanian authorities were fixed on making an example of him to deter other would-be poachers. But he claims no-one else is willing to risk death running small boats across the most dangerous stretch of water in the southern hemisphere. 'It's too hard,' he says. 'Since I stopped, where are they? No-one is crossing Bass Strait to dive because it's serious stuff, like climbing Everest without oxygen.'

So much for the past. As for the future, Strachan says he can let go of the fast money but not the fast boats. He is proud of his boat-building, and delighted that the Tasmanian police share his confidence: they have used a boat he built in his backyard ever since they confiscated it in 1997.

This opens up the potential for his own version of poacher-turned-gamekeeper. His client list already includes people like television fishing guru Rex Hunt, and now the lion wants to lie down with the lamb ... he has a standing offer to Fisheries officers and water police to test any government craft against his home-grown 'Formula Extreme' prototype: 'If they can outperform one of mine in rough water, I will supply one for nothing'.

Meanwhile, he has finally learned that you can't beat City Hall. He wants to be around to see his twins grow up. Maybe even take them fishing one day ... but only with a rod and reel, he told the author in early 2005. Strachan swears he is a reformed character, but an appeal court did not see it that way. In August 2005 he was sentenced to ten months jail, with the threat of another suspended sentence also looming that could keep him in prison for eighteen months. By the time he gets out, his baby twins will be walking and perhaps even talking. Boats and money are not the only things he has lost.

ANYONE who has survived years of abalone diving needs luck, especially if crossing Bass Strait regularly in conditions considered too dangerous for Fisheries officers, water police and licensed fishermen. Many remarkable stories have become lore. One that can now be told concerns a sometime pub bouncer-turned-poacher who currently leads a quiet life in Tasmania after surviving terrifying odds. Because of a usually-fatal combination of recklessness, greed and a Bass Strait storm, the poacher and his two young crewmates were caught in killer seas in a small boat in late 1998 while trying to run back to Victoria from the small islands off the north-west corner of Tasmania. The poacher had set off the boat's emergency satellite beacon far too late to be rescued by conventional means. He was too foolhardy to sound the mayday alarm early because he was reluctant to jettison the load of abalone; until it was too late.

Just when it seemed certain that he would lose this insane gamble and that he and his mates would be drowned, salvation arrived in the unlikely form of a passing US Navy battleship, one of few craft big enough to brave a Bass Strait storm with relative impunity.

The battleship had been serving in the Gulf and was steaming along the Australian coast to visit Melbourne when it picked up the distress signal and diverted course to search for the stricken fishing boat.

After a tense and dangerous rescue the three shaken, half-frozen and grateful men were dragged on board and placed in the sick bay, where they were plied with soup, cigarettes and curious questions about what the hell they thought they were doing in the middle of one of the world's most dangerous stretches of water in a glorified plastic runabout. Well before they reached Port Melbourne, the poacher skipper had recovered well enough from the ordeal to work out that the authorities would be waiting for him with difficult questions – and perhaps handcuffs. Determined to snatch victory from the jaws of defeat, he turned his considerable charm on the battle-ship's bemused officers, impressing them with tales of working the Strait and the injustice of the system.

When the battleship docked, Fisheries officers and water police requested permission to come aboard and interview the rescued 'fishermen'. But the American captain promptly refused, pointing out that his ship was technically United States soil and that they had no authority to board it, let alone arrest anyone.

Being trained strategists, the Americans knew how to avoid a stalemate and pre-empt a possible siege situation with a decisive tactical decision. They quietly bundled the three poachers into a small helicopter and landed them on a quiet beach at Seaford, where they were met by friends in a car. For the second time in 48 hours, they were the ones that got away.

The poacher skipper learned his lesson, according to Cam Strachan, who knows him well. Realising he could not afford to tempt fate again, he leads a quiet life on a salmon farm, never more than swimming distance from shore.

ABALONE diving is risky, abalone poaching even more so. But not all poachers are reckless. A few discreet operators have never been caught and remain unknown. Others might be suspected but stay out of trouble. One of them – 'Jim' – lives in the house that abalone built on the farm that abalone bought in a remote and beautiful part of Victoria's west coast. Jim describes himself drily as an 'ethical poacher' – and in the past tense. He says he gave up poaching after a few lucrative years because of the increased policing and massive rise in penalties which put abalone and lobster trafficking in the same league as drug trafficking.

But even when he was diving for abalone, he says, he did not strip beds, take huge catches, or take undersized abalone. In all ways, except the lack of a licence, he behaved the way that legitimate abalone divers should. He says he always went 'softly softly' – and had the discipline to give it up once he had set himself up so that he could pursue less dangerous pursuits.

As a young man he was a good sportsman, and he came to western Victoria to play football. He worked in a local business with an older man who introduced him to abalone diving off Warrnambool, Port Fairy and Portland.

The shellfish wasn't worth nearly as much then, but it was plentiful – the old timers called it 'mutton fish' and reckoned it was good for bait – but even back then a few hours diving could get him half a week's wages. The older man bought a licence for a few dollars and urged young Jim to do the same. 'He used to say to me "buy a licence, there'll be money in this one day". He's a multi-millionaire now.'

Jim sounds a bit wistful but says he has no regrets. He didn't see the missed opportunity until it was too late – and didn't care when he was young. By the time he realised that abalone could have made him rich too, he felt he couldn't justify the cost of going 'legit'. Each time the price of licences rose, he thought it was too expensive to take the plunge. When the authorities imposed a $200 licence fee in the mid-1970s – about two weeks ordinary wages – it shook scores of divers out of the game, which was the intended effect.

Those who decided $200 was too much outlay sold out to those hardier and farsighted divers who had to comply with a new ruling that they needed to buy two licences in order to consolidate them into one. Within months, the number of licensed divers halved – and the foundations had been laid for a closed shop of a few dozen potential millionaires. Every time the licences changed hands for more and more money, the harder it seemed for Jim and others like him to justify coming up with the money. Instead, he says, he started poaching regularly. The secret of his modest success, he says, was that he wasn't greedy. 'I was an ethical sort of poacher,' he muses. 'I only took sized abalone and went into areas the professionals wouldn't.'

In those days, regional Fisheries officers were scarce and

fairly regular in their habits. Jim would always go out before dawn or after dark. In the mid- 1980s, he was getting about $14 a kilogram for abalone, mostly from trusted clients who ran Chinese restaurants. In three busy years, he made enough to buy several acres of prime coastal land and to build a house. A few hours diving would subsidise several days of building. When he finished the house and had everything paid off, he says, he walked away from poaching.

'I had a goal and achieved that goal,' he says. Not everyone is so wise.

Of course, it takes nerve just to dive some of the reefs. Around Julia Percy Island, where the great white sharks hunt seal pups, for instance. 'I know a few who have lost their nerve,' says the modest poacher. But the days are gone when you could 'set your watch' by the Fisheries officers starting and stopping work. 'I would never dive in office hours', he explains. Now policing is much more stringent.

Jim isn't the only poacher to quit while ahead. A lot of other poachers have 'pulled up' because of the savage penalties abalone (and lobster) trafficking carry. A repeat offender caught with a trafficable quantity could get nearly as much jail time as a 'cleanskin' first offender might get for manslaughter. They can also have assets seized and sold under draconian provisions that treat abalone poachers like drug dealers. There are men in every coastal community who have lost cars, boats and diving equipment to the Fisheries officers.

The tough new laws are particularly discouraging for the sophisticated 'boat poachers' like Cam Strachan and others, who use expensive, high-powered boats – often custom made – fitted with air compressors to supply air to divers through 'hookah' air lines. Some poachers use expensive imported 're-breathing' equipment – painted in camouflage colours to match camouflage wetsuits – which does not release tell-tale bubbles to the surface.

Big boat poachers who stand to make big money fast are rarely seen on the job by the public. These offenders, in the slang used by Fisheries officers, are mostly 'corkies' – Caucasian – whereas organised teams of shore poachers tend to be Asian. The latter stand out to the public because they arrive in carloads to hit accessible areas at low tide to duck-dive on shallow reefs, mostly in daylight. These bogus 'recreational' divers exploit a legal loophole: breaking the spirit if not the letter of the law by taking the recreational limit of ten abalone a day, every day that they can.

They take more if they can get away with it, stashing their catch in the tea-tree to be retrieved later, then going back in for another bag. If they are caught with only a few over the limit, they avoid full-scale trafficking charges. It is not unknown for them to bring extra carloads of 'mules' – children and old people – who each return to the suburbs clutching their 'catch' of ten abalone each.

The big risks – physical and legal – are taken by divers working at night, either from shore using scuba tanks or from boats. These offenders can take substantial catches, risking trafficking charges to cash in on black market prices of up to $50 a kilogram for abalone meat. Some can make $5000 in a night.

A serious poacher who doesn't get caught could theoretically make close to a million dollars cash in a year. But most do get caught.

The combination of big money and willingness to risk jail attracts a criminal element that is a long way from the 'respectable' local poachers like Jim.

THE ruthless tag-team approach by the organised gangs of recreational poachers in the tidal zones within two hours of Melbourne is a death of a thousand cuts for once-plentiful recreational abalone stocks close to shore. In the quiet roads in the tea-tree hugging the ocean beaches on the Mornington Peninsula, the locals can easily pick the shore poachers' cars. They are almost always early model Commodores or Falcons – cheap, disposable and relatively anonymous, with plenty of room to carry five passengers and a boot full of abalone back to suburbs like Springvale and Oakleigh, where they are quietly sold to restaurants or illegally processed for sale – often to Asian tourists who prize the shellfish.

Locals, notably male surfers, wage a silent guerrilla war with the shore poachers. They let down tyres, kick in panels and smash windows but they don't want to identify themselves in print because of potential repercussions.

Ken de Heer has run the kiosk at Sorrento back beach for ten years, and has seen the suburban poachers turn up in increasing numbers every time the weather and tide are suitable – meaning a northerly wind blowing offshore and a low tide. He says these 'tidal zone' poachers now leave someone minding their cars. Four wear wetsuits and blue kitchen gloves and carry mesh onion bags; one watches the car to stop vigilante locals disabling it.

The 'sentry' often carries a spear gun or diving knife. A lot of locals are nervous of them.

'In the beginning there was a lot of anger and angst when they would come back up from the beach to the car park with their bags full,' de Heer explains. After a series of clashes between surfers and poachers 'we were told to back off and get car (registration) numbers.' The poachers have taken to avoiding the main car parks, although the locals can pick their cars along back beach roads.

Simon is a Sorrento local in his 40s who swims in the surf every day. He is tanned, fit, stocky and angry, in a laid-back way. He sees the same faces and the same cars month after month when tide and winds suit. 'They walk in, wearing wetsuits and goggles and a bum bag. They travel pretty light. I took some photos once. Later on, we got our tyres slashed. I can't say it was them (the poachers) but I reckon it was because the surfers let their tyres down. It's a bit of a silent war.

'Twenty years ago you used to put your hands under the rocks and pull the abs off, and there were shellfish all over the peninsula. But now it's all gone.' He points to a big abalone shell sitting on a table on his verandah. 'That size used to be common,' he says, 'but you could dive all day now to find one that big around here.' He is referring specifically to the beaches accessible from shore. Not all shore poachers are Asian, he adds. 'An Aussie bloke was doing a fair bit of poaching here. He saw me looking at him and he said "I know where you live, so don't say anything".'

POACHERS were always good at hiding abalone but, as fines increased and authorities began confiscating cars, boats and equipment, their scams have grown more elaborate. One former poacher – now a car dealer – showed the author a modified scuba tank, with a small air reservoir at the top but able to be filled with abalone through a false bottom.

Other ruses include gutted 'spare' outboard motors containing abalone instead of engines, hollow life jackets with hidden zips, dummy fuel tanks and secret compartments in boats. David Strachan's cruiser *Janthe* had one such compartment that could hide three illegal divers who were willing to lie underneath an enormous water tank that slid on hidden tracks.

Some gangs have been known to cut open fibreglass decks with compressed-air-driven power tools, fill the hollow hull with abalone, then re-cover the hole and throw the tools overboard before returning to port.

For years, one illegal abalone gang used an ice-cream delivery truck fitted with a powerful motor to collect abalone from poachers along the Victorian coast. 'The ice-cream in the back of the truck was about two years old,' says an insider whose family has worked the fish markets for two generations. 'But the abalone was always fresh.' A 'runner' was recently caught with a utility converted to a giant icebox, with insulation panels fitted to the bottom and sides. Another Victorian gang used cars fitted with LP gas so the petrol tanks could be used to carry abalone. It worked well until officers smelt something fishy.

Large-scale poaching depends on a ready market. There is a difference between selling a few abalone to the local Chinese restaurant and a large-scale criminal enterprise.

As long as there are processors – illegal ones without licences or unethical ones with a licence – there will be a few people willing to run the risk of poaching and running abalone. Which is why the authorities – Fisheries and police – are combining forces to crack the processors. This is the story of their greatest success so far...

LIKE many another Asian businessman, Tat Sang Loo is – or was – a gambler. He was not a high roller at casinos or card games but he played for high stakes. He bet against his liberty, and lost. If anyone knows who dobbed him in, it's a well-kept secret. Later, the Fisheries people would say only that they thought it was an anonymous tip-off, which is as likely a story as any.

It's not as if Tat Sang Loo was a known organised crime figure – although he was certainly committing a crime and was admirably organised, one reason his backyard abalone empire was so easy to unravel once the investigators got a sniff that it existed. A sniff, in fact, might have been Tat Sang's undoing. He was drying abalone in the roof of his neat clinker brick house in Calembeena Street, Oakleigh, in Melbourne's outer eastern suburbs.

The drying shellfish gave off a distinctive smell. Not an unpleasant odour, recalls the pleasant elderly woman who still lives next door. 'It wasn't a fishy smell,' she says, 'more sweet, like baking biscuits.'

Smell or no smell, it was a fishy business. Tat Sang Loo was in his 40s, married twice and with a young family. He had been a restaurant worker – manager or kitchen hand, depending on who's telling the story – when fortune seemed to smile on him. He was home a lot, and started buying properties. Neighbours noticed that he was also becoming popular. People visited at all hours of day. And they brought 'gifts' in heavy-duty plastic bags.

By the time the Fisheries surveillance crew sat off Tat Sang Loo's house, his social circle had expanded even further. The watchers followed his Commodore station wagon to a series of quiet suburban car parks, where he would do 'tail-to-tail' pick ups of the heavy black bags from other cars. Often, he would then go to a rundown weatherboard house tucked behind a commercial building on a busy main road a few blocks from his own home in Oakleigh.

The surveillance crew noticed that when the station wagon entered the driveway it well loaded down but later emerged (from behind tall gates) empty, riding much higher on its springs. At other times, it arrived empty and left loaded with sealed cardboard boxes. They got lucky one day, when the 'target' parked at a shopping centre and left the car briefly. Officers swiftly broke into it and opened one of the boxes. It was full of dried abalone.

The boxes were addressed to Sydney and Queensland and had stickers that identified a local road freight company, which meant that when our abalone runner got to the transport depot to unload, the investigators were already waiting for him, hidden with cameras ready.

After that, it was all over bar the shouting. There was plenty of that when about 60 Fisheries officers and police divided into teams raided four properties in Oakleigh and Huntingdale on a spring day in 1998. The investigators were well-briefed but surprised by what they found in one of them – the shabby weatherboard at 2 Leigh Street, Huntingdale, was fitted out inside like a professional processing plant. The living areas were sheathed in stainless steel and fitted with industrial kitchen benches, cryovac sealing machines, and a row of washing machines to tumble the abalone meat. A room fitted with a gas furnace was full of drying racks loaded with abalone. There were freezers full of abalone.

Among papers at the scene was a receipt that led the investigators to a self-storage depot in a nearby industrial estate. There they found boxes of dried abalone, a cache stored to send interstate.

The haul totalled 31,004 abalone – the biggest in Australia, before or since. When Tat Sang Loo appeared in court later, the prosecution led evidence that he had grossed $1.2 million in the year before his arrest and had an interest in five properties, including a city apartment and a new brick house.

The judge ordered him to pay $978,275 under the Confiscation Act of 1997, and sentenced him to more than a year in prison. Meanwhile, it seemed, he was also unlucky in love. His wife filed for divorce as soon as he was arrested, which meant she was entitled to half his considerable assets.

Fisheries officers believe she managed to keep their impressive new house in one of the best streets in East Oakleigh. It is opposite a school and has tall, black security gates that slide open and shut automatically as soon as a car comes or goes.

If you watch the house long enough, they say, you can still see a man who uncannily resembles Tat Sang Loo slipping in and out.

Perhaps he and his wife have managed to reconcile. Crime might have paid a bit, after all.

He's extremely cunning, very patient and very, very deadly

– from Billy Longley's police file

8.
THE SHOOTIST

ON the waterfront they called it the 'apple cucumber' but it wasn't health food. It was gangster slang for a deadly double cross that works like this: a false friend lures the target to a meeting that turns into an ambush when a third party arrives, armed and unannounced. That's the sneaky way they nearly got Billy 'The Texan' Longley in 1971. But he was too smart for them.

Longley got a call from Alfred 'The Ferret' Nelson, social secretary of the painters and dockers union, a job description that covered a lot of ground. Nelson asked Longley to meet him in the Webb Dock mess room, where waterfront workers sometimes ate their lunch and always minded their own business, even if they happened to get spattered with blood.

Longley had to sit with his back to the swinging doors

because his host was already seated, facing him across the long mess table. Longley gently slid his handgun out of his belt and, as they chatted about union business, aimed it underneath the table at Nelson. In his business, it was insurance.

The small talk stopped when Longley heard the doors swish behind him. He cocked the hidden pistol and turned to see who was coming. It wasn't good. Jack Twist, famed on the docks for croaking the notorious standover man Freddy 'The Frog' Harrison years before, was approaching fast. He had his hands deep in his overalls pockets and a look on his face that said he had a gun in each of them.

This, Longley observed later with studied understatement, was 'a fairly serious situation.'

But Longley had an advantage: Nelson had heard him cock the gun and realised any hostile move by Twist meant getting shot. 'When I cocked my piece "The Ferret" went white,' Longley was to recall. 'He was a nano-second from death. He said "Bill! Give me a chance – let me talk to him" and he got up and ran up to Twist and threw his arms around him so he couldn't get his guns out of his pockets. Then he took him outside. I should have shot 'em both then and there,' he adds in disgust. Time hasn't dulled some old hatreds.

'The Ferret' saved himself that day – but not for long. He disappeared from his Collingwood lodging soon after, just before the painters and dockers union election in December 1971 that erupted into an open gunfight, a public battle in a long-running guerRilla war in which perhaps dozens of 'dockies' died and many more were injured.

Police were to winch Nelson's car from the water near South Wharf but he was not in it. Much later, a detective standing on a new concrete ramp on the dock was told 'Watch it, you're standing on "The Ferret".' Nelson's body was never found. But there was no doubt, as Longley deadpanned later, that he had 'given up smoking and drinking.' And he wasn't the only one on the missing list.

'It was self preservation,' Longley says, quiet but unrepentant. 'Get in first, before they get you.'

So much for Longley the gunslinger. What about the man? He is rather more complicated. He has been a pigeon fancier, skilled tradesman, bull-mastiff dog breeder, ballroom dancer, committed unionist, hack golfer and handy tennis player, a patient father to his only daughter and grandfather to her children.

Accused (and later convicted) of shooting a painters and dockers union secretary, he had the cunning and the contacts to hide from his underworld enemies and police for sixteen months before turning himself in. He had the willpower to give up smoking in jail – and to lose 30 kilograms at Weight Watchers after getting out. He had the personality to partner a former policeman to persuade delinquent teenagers to mend their ways and errant debtors to pay their way. He reads military histories, biographies and *The Age* newspaper and plays Scrabble.

And lately, every morning, he does water aerobics with a group of respectable older women who won't hear a bad word about their Bill.

Times change. In the 1950s, Longley's favourite water sport was tossing beer cans in the Murray River and shooting them with a pistol as they floated past. He made himself a good shot – one reason he grew old when so many of his contemporaries didn't.

'I've had blokes miss me with six shots from two car lengths away,' he recalls. 'But I didn't miss many.' He almost smiles.

Because of the dockers' code of silence most such incidents

were never made public. But one showdown was later aired in court. It happened on a Saturday night in July 1968 at the Rose and Crown Hotel in Port Melbourne after one John Robert Waymouth made the mistake of abusing Billy's partner, Barbara, after accidentally bumping her.

Waymouth was grabbed from behind by several willing hands and tossed out of the bar and onto the street. He was given a belting and left in the gutter as a lesson in etiquette. When Waymouth revived, he made another mistake: he wanted revenge. He called his two sons, who turned up with three friends to even the score.

In the ensuing brawl, guns were produced. At least, one gun was – the one that did all the damage. The result was that five men ended up with .45 calibre bullet wounds, mostly in the buttocks. Two of them decided not to press charges.

Longley heard that the police wanted to question him over the shooting of three men. Five days later he presented himself – with his lawyer, the legendary Frank Galbally – at South Melbourne police station. He was charged on three counts apiece of wounding with intent to murder and grievous bodily harm.

The case against him looked strong but it soon sprang leaks. For a start, only Waymouth was willing to claim that Longley had fired the shots. The other witnesses, including the wounded, seemed unsure what had happened. One even said he did not think Longley had fired the shots.

The clincher came from the courtroom genius of 'The Silver Fox', Galbally, who smoothly led Waymouth into the trap of admitting that the police had shown him a picture of Longley in their efforts to identify him as the shooter. There was, as Galbally and the judge knew, a legal precedent that unless a witness had selected a picture of the supposed guilty party from several photographs of different people, it was inadmissible. The case was dismissed. And another chapter in the intertwined stories of the legendary lawyer and his valued client, Billy Longley, became lore.

For a long time after that, if Galbally had any problems in his chambers with cranky clients or bad debtors, Longley would drop in and sort it out. 'If ever I had a hurdle to jump, I always went to Mr Frank,' he said later. 'He protected me from the slings and arrows.'

THEY called him 'The Texan' because, the story goes, he wore a big Stetson hat and carried a Colt .45 pistol. Longley disputes this. 'The hat wasn't that big,' he growls, face as sombre as a well-kept grave.

In fact, the nickname came from a TV western series, *The Texan*, made from 1958 to 1960, when Longley was a towering figure on the waterfront, feared nearly as much in Sydney as he was in Melbourne. The show starred a laconic hero coincidentally called Bill Longley, who wouldn't be pushed around by bad guys and was polite to women folk: an irresistible role model for a well-dressed man about town who liked dancing and shooting.

'The Texan' is 80 now, one of few to survive the Melbourne dock wars that, as he points out with a historical flourish, inflicted more casualties than the Eureka Rebellion – around 40 men dead and many more wounded during a decade that spawned the now-notorious saying, 'We catch and kill our own.'

The Federated Painters and Dockers Union was a closed shop, harder to get into than The Melbourne Stock Exchange. Members joined by invitation based on their reputation. Longley, a wharfie for 17 years, became a 'dockie' in 1967. Of around 360 members, 200 had serious criminal records.

It was only natural, he says, that men with criminal records who could not get jobs elsewhere would end up in the few jobs where a record was not held against them. It was self-selection. Longley's friend, the feared former policeman Brian Murphy, points out that there was a Vagrancy Act in those days, which meant that anyone without a job or visible means of support could be thrown in jail at the whim of police and magistrates. One answer to that was to join a waterside union, therefore getting on the roster for casual work.

Not that it was easy to get a job on the Melbourne wharves. In his book, Longley describes a remarkable scene of working class history:

You went and appeared at the West Melbourne stadium (Festival Hall) where all the fights took place and you walked on the stage under the arc lights in front of all these blokes so that they could take a look at you. You were tested for soundness., and if you were undesirable they might yell out 'YOU! You bludger – you repossessed my sister's refrigerator, you rotten bastard!' They didn't want undesirables – so if you were a police informer, a child molester or a debt collector you didn't stand a chance. You'd be booed out of the hall and the union and be lucky, as the saying went, 'to escape with your ears'. You'd have to come pretty well recommended to get a job on the wharves – they were men's men, the cream of the crop.

Not that Longley had any trouble with scrutiny under the bright lights at the 'House of Stoush'. Having passed muster with his peers, he was warned by the chairman of the Stevedoring Industry Board that he was 'on probation' because of his police record.

'Don't think you're coming down here to steal, fight or be playing up in any way,' the chairman warned him on his first day. Longley assured him he was just after a steady job. It is true that in the next three decades he was not always a stranger to stealing and fighting. But along the way he made lifelong friends with many ordinary wharfies who were not criminals, but working-class men supporting their families the best way they could. Such friendships with 'cleanskins' would save his life later, when he 'went into smoke' to avoid both the police and his enemies in the rival painters and dockers faction.

Longley was invited to be a painter and docker in 1967. It was, he knew, because he had a reputation as a 'gunnie' that would be useful to those who sponsored him into the union. Men like him were insurance for union organisers who did not want to be pushed around.

The reality was that there was a quiet but deadly war between rival groups of gangsters intent on controlling the union and, therefore, lucrative rackets such as 'ghosting' (picking up pay packets for nonexistent workers), systematic pilfering and smuggling. Some 'dockies' also indulged in armed robbery, illegal gambling and standover rackets. Whoever controlled the docks effectively controlled organised crime in Australia.

Later, in 1980, an exposé by *The Bulletin* magazine led to the Costigan royal commission into waterfront corruption, which exposed rackets that had tentacles reaching into every level of society – from drug running to illegal gambling and, notably, 'bottom-of-the-harbour' tax rorts exploited by supposedly legitimate business people.

Longley was no angel, and liked easy money as much as the next gunman, but unlike a lot of career criminals he had been a genuine worker and was proud of it: he had served an apprenticeship as a tradesman and had spent his formative years working in industry, as had his father.

He has never wavered from his claim that when he stood as union president in December 1971 it was on a genuine reform ticket to protect ordinary members. In his view, then and now, the battlers who did the dirty, dangerous work on the docks had been sold out by greedy union leaders willing to enrich themselves by doing corrupt deals with shipping lines.

Longley has always insisted he won the vote – one of the vote counters told him he'd 'shit it in' – but, after a gun battle, the ballot box was stolen and voting slips were destroyed. This outrage rankled and almost certainly led to his brave and perhaps foolhardy decision ultimately to brief the journalist who wrote the *Bulletin* expose and, subsequently, to give evidence to the Costigan commission about the rackets that would eventually lead to the union being deregistered in 1993.

But that was later.

DESPITE the Hollywood nickname, Longley is a reminder of a vanished Australia: the sort of man once seen at RSL clubs and in the betting ring at the races, shaped by 1930s austerity, stern Victorian forebears and a predominantly Ango-Celtic society.

At a glance, he could be any respectable retired grandfather. He would not look out of place at the Lions Club, on a racing club committee, even in church. When he goes out, he wears a dark suit, white shirt and perfectly knotted tie, and gleaming black shoes. Fingernails clean and clipped. Grey hair combed. He always had presence. Dignity, even.

He has none of the stereotype markers of the criminal underclass: no tattoos, little jewellery, no addiction to gambling, alcohol or drugs. He is gruff but not rough, with a courtliness few would mistake for weakness.

If he were ever a swashbuckler, that has long gone; now he looks somewhere between Alfred Hitchcock and the old gunfighter played by John Wayne in his last film, *The Shootist*, doing what a man has to do before the final ride to Boot Hill.

There are a few waiting for him there. It has been said for 30 years that Longley was the last to see several of his waterfront opponents alive; legend suggests as many as 15.

Certainly, his lawyers once told him police threatened to charge him with seven murders. Longley vehemently denies any part of killing painters and dockers union secretary Pat Shannon in 1973 – for which he was later jailed – but is quiet about other deaths. To be fair, he is silent about most things from his past. He speaks only when he has something to say, sticking grimly to a code of silence that, at his age, has all but lost its relevance.

Most of the stories he could tell would be about dead men, as he has virtually outlived his generation of crims and knockabouts, dockies and wharfies, and a group of tough and corrupt police who used fists, handcuffs and guns to extract their dues from the underworld in the name of law and order.

He says his fearsome reputation was 'like wearing a hair shirt', though he concedes it had some advantages. For instance, it might have saved his life in jail – though probably put him there in the first place.

Dead men tell no tales and for most of his life, neither has Longley. Once, his idea of a long sentence was 13 years for murder – which is the time he served over the Shannon shooting. But since agreeing to a book about his life – his biography *In Your Face* was launched in July 2005 – he is warming to the talking business. Sometimes he puts several sentences together. But not often.

'I get sick of talking about myself,' he told the authors in a frank moment. 'It shits me'. In the past, in his line of work, silence suited him. He found Teddy Roosevelt's injunction – to speak softly and carry a big stick – more effective.

At his 80th birthday dinner at the Royal Hotel in Essendon,

the new talkative Billy Longley spoke for at least three minutes. Perhaps two. 'I look around and see good faces, kind faces,' he began gravely, as his only daughter Lisa took snaps of the eclectic gathering. 'I only mix with good people these days.'

He mentioned several guests by name – starting with his biographer, journalist Rochelle Jackson, a policeman's daughter who first met him while researching a television current affairs story a decade ago, and started on the book in 2003. Another guest was a retired Pentridge prison governor, Jim Armstrong, who later told the crowd that in jail Longley 'was a straight stick in a pile of debris' and a man who 'walked his own line'.

Longley says he has 'Catholic tastes' in friends as well as interests, a point underlined by the gathering at his birthday. Playing the violin and leading the singing at the party was a former journalist who advises the Liberal Party on tactics and policy. Singing along was Dean Mighell, hard-nosed leader of the Electrical Trades Union, who grew up in the northern suburbs knowing the Longley legend.

Other guests included Brian Francis Murphy, a renowned former policeman who became friendly with Longley after refusing to give trumped-up evidence against him over the shooting of five men in the Rose and Crown Hotel. After Longley left prison in 1988, Murphy joined him in a trouble-shooting mediation business with the motto 'everything can be negotiated.' Their specialty was debt collecting and persuading wayward teenagers to avoid a life of crime. They were considered most persuasive. Often a business card in a letter box was enough to bring a speedy resolution to problems.

Also at the birthday party was one of Billy's brothers, Reg Longley, looking the respectable retired barber he is in reefer jacket, cardigan and spectacles. Others included the couple who ran the Moonee Ponds coffee shop where Longley sat at the same table for years, greeting a stream of friends most mornings. For a long time the couple knew the polite older man only as 'Bill' and didn't realise his notoriety until his picture was in the newspaper one morning. Then they understood why so many older locals – men and women – came in and shook hands or kissed him. He was the Godfather of Puckle Street.

The café has changed hands recently, and Longley has switched allegiance to another one in Ascot Vale, around the corner from his flat.

Phillip Adams – broadcaster, film-maker, columnist, stirrer – didn't get to Billy's birthday party. He now only occasionally corresponds with Longley, but his observations of the man he sometimes visited in prison 25 years ago are still vivid. Adams, then an *Age* columnist, received thousands of letters a year but he sensed a powerful personality in a note Longley wrote to him from Pentridge in the late 1970s. That – and, he cheerfully admits, Longley's notoriety – drew him to visit and to write to him and about him. He did, after all, have a column to fill and Longley needed a voice in the world outside jail, so they suited each other's purposes. Something they both recognise in each other.

Adams was streetwise enough to be wary of being manipulated by 'a highly intelligent man'. But at his first sight of Longley, in a security cage used for prison visits in Pentridge's H division, he was struck by 'this charming, likable avuncular gentleman with all this violence swirling around him like a mist'. Curious, Adams asked barrister friends about Longley's conviction for Shannon's murder 'and the consensus was he didn't do it but had done plenty of others'.

It was the beginning of an odd friendship between the cultured and affluent intellectual and a middle-aged gunman surviving in a prison system where any one of many younger men might have killed him for reputation or reward. Longley had his ways of surviving. One was to mind his own business, and to let the mystique that had grown around him work its effect. He gave no offence but he gave the impression that anyone who interfered with him was 'in for seven years bad luck, that's for sure'.

Often, as a billet trusted to mop floors in Pentridge, he was called on to mop up blood spilt after officers 'flogged' a prisoner with batons. A senior officer quietly said to him one day, 'This won't happen to you, will it Bill? We know you'd even up.' It was a case of the reputation that put him inside protecting him while he was there. A double-edged sword.

Reputation wasn't quite enough. Longley's strong personality helped him get what he wanted. He once persuaded Phillip Adams to drive to Ararat prison, two hours from Melbourne, to give him a set of golf clubs. When Adams saw him there he was reminded of 'an old caged lion living carefully' among younger prisoners. What he didn't know was that the old lion still had teeth: he had a pistol stashed inside the jail, just in case.

The funny thing was, years later Longley was talking to a retired prison officer who told him the prison staff had known he had a pistol hidden somewhere.

Adams says he has interviewed possibly 20,000 people 'and I forget most of them before they're out of the room – but I've never forgotten Billy'. He was intrigued by what he calls 'the cognitive dissonance between what he did ... and the sort of rather sweet guy he seemed to be'.

Adams was describing Longley as he was in his 50s. At 80, the dissonance between the dignified old man and his menacing reputation is even more striking. For his birthday, Longley dressed in Sunday best – conservative grey suit, white shirt,

Crocodile tears … John Sharpe pleads for his wife and child to 'come home'. He'd killed them weeks earlier.

The Sharpes at a family picnic … was he already planning double murder?

Beyond belief … police search for the butchered remains of mother and child.

In Loving Memory of

Anna Marie Kemp

1962 – 2004

In Loving Memory of

Gracie Louise Sharpe

2002 – 2004

Dressed to kill … Billy Longley deep in thought outside court.

The wrong iron … loner Longley works on his game at the exclusive Bluestone Country Club.

**Hits and memories … Billy Longley, the Godfather of
Moonee Ponds.**

muted tie, polished shoes. He is not tall and his stocky figure has ballooned recently because ageing legs no longer allow him to play golf or tennis or follow his lifelong passion for ballroom dancing. His hands are manicured. In dress and manner he could be a retired country bank manager at a family wedding. Almost.

The only hint of his past is a hard streak, like an old army sergeant who has seen battle and is used to command. Which, had things been slightly different, he might have been.

HE was born in 1925, second son and fourth child of eight belonging to Wilfred and Elizabeth Longley, who had arrived in Australia after World War I just in time for the Depression. He says he was christened 'Billy' rather than 'William' because it was his mother's pet name for her favourite brother.

Wilfred Longley was a Yorkshireman, a fitter and turner who had served as a Navy petty officer in the war and had married up the social scale when he wed Elizabeth Holbest Roxburgh, a Scottish school teacher from the Isle of Lewis, and daughter of a naval commander. If Elizabeth had hoped Australia promised something better than a bleak Scottish island for her growing family, she was disappointed. Wilfred had to chase work, sometimes interstate, while she coped with a series of mean rented houses in Melbourne's working-class west.

When Longley says the Depression and poverty pushed him into a life of crime, a listener can tell he's sung the same song so often he might even believe it himself. As with most beliefs, it must have sprung from a grain of truth. But he admits that his surviving siblings (two sisters died in childhood, an emotional scar he avoids talking about) grew up as respectable 'square-heads', embarrassed by his lawlessness. To hear him interpret his own life story, it seems that hardship sharpened a rebellious streak in him that his brothers and sisters did not have. He fought for survival and begged and stole to eat as a boy, then got to like it.

He traces his hatred of authority to the day a conductor kicked him in the face as he clung to the side of the tram for a free ride. 'My face hit the tram track and I skidded along, finishing in a bloody mess.' He recalls a passing motorist picking him up, bleeding, from the gutter and taking him home.

There were other turning points. He remembers the day his father got into a brawl with a neighbour and was being badly beaten. 'I ran to the toolbox and grabbed a hammer and hit him (the other man) in the kidneys as hard as I could,' says Longley. Then he hit him in the head. Although his father preached 'tact and diplomacy' to his sons, his actions sent a different message. He took the boy to a pub, rewarded his loyalty with praise, oysters and porter gaff. And so he learned at an impressionable age that violence paid off – a lesson hard to unlearn.

Longley clearly loved his mother, and inherited her love of reading, but he admits evading her efforts to steer him away from trouble. From the little he says, and much he doesn't, emerges a picture of a worn-out and homesick woman, disappointed by her lot, heartbroken at the loss of two daughters and the lack of opportunity for her other children. Longley doesn't criticise his father, but the implication is clear: it wasn't a happy household.

On Sundays, he says, he would suggest that his mother read in bed while he cooked a roast dinner for the family. She quoted poetry to him that he can still recite a lifetime later and she told him he was 'fey' – had the intuition of her Celtic forebears. He believed this sixth sense saved his life, later. But it didn't keep him out of trouble.

He was expelled from Ascot Vale primary school in sixth

grade for punching a teacher who threatened to strap his younger sister, Peggy.

He had already been in trouble for stealing cigarettes from a shop. In early 1937, he got 12 months probation for shoplifting. In late 1938, he was sent to a boys' home for attempted shop breaking.

By the time he got out, war was looming and employment booming. The Depression was over. His father started work at the ordnance factory at Maribyrnong and got him a fitting and turning apprenticeship. Young Billy liked work. It might have been a stabilising influence but any harmony was shattered when his mother's father fell ill in Britain; despite the war, Mrs Longley got a passage 'home' to nurse the old navy man.

Billy was 15, and scared his mother might not get back. He describes how the family stood on the dock, crying, as her ship steamed away. They watched it until it became a dot and disappeared over the horizon. It was the end of his childhood.

Billy and two of the other children went to board with other families and his father looked after the other three. He was treated well and speaks fondly of the family he stayed with, but adolescence was not a good time to be missing his mother's influence.

He bought a shotgun from a workmate, took up rabbit shooting and fantasised about what he would do if the 'Japs' invaded. Even 65 years on, his face hardens as he relives the fears of that uncertain time. 'The first one down the hallway was going to get his head blown off, that's for sure,' he says.

He did well at work, making anti-aircraft guns, but he was on 'starvation' apprentice wages – a sixth of a tradesman's wage – and dabbled in minor crime to raise spending money. To his joy, his mother returned safely in 1943 with an inheritance from the death of her father the old Naval officer. She bought a house in

Essendon and the family was reunited. But by this time her Billy had a bad name with the local police and there was nothing she could do.

When he turned 18, he tried to enlist in the local drill hall but was refused because his work making guns was vital to the war effort. As more of his dance hall and work mates joined up, he tried twice more.

After the third attempt, his boss called him away from his lathe and into his office at the ordnance factory and read the riot act. He warned him that even if he managed to bluff his way into the services and onto a troopship, he would be sent back from the Middle East because his job was worth 'three or four soldiers'.

He often wondered, later, how his life would have turned out had he got into the army. He fancies that war might have suited him more than most. If there was one thing that stood out about him later, he was cool under fire.

As it was, he worked hard all week but was a weekend tearaway who waged a private war with the local police after making the mistake of beating one constable in a street fight. The inevitable payback for this unpardonable offence was to be thrown in the cells and beaten up by several police, obliged to back up their colleague.

Those were the rules on the streets of Ascot Vale in the 1940s. It was to have lasting effects.

When the war ended and the munitions factory wound down, Longley was a skilled tradesman. He still has his set of framed indentures and is proud of them. But he claims he lost three engineering jobs in quick succession because police warned employers against him. So he retreated into the 'knockabout' world. He spent six months working in a rabbit-skinning works then moved up to a job on the wharves. By then he was carrying a pistol. He had been a street fighter – 'all in, no boxing' – since he was at primary school. One afternoon in his late teens, he says, 'I had the good luck to run against three blokes and get over the top (defeat) of all of them. That night I went to the pictures, and I saw one of them. He looked at me and pulled back his jacket so I could see what he had stuck in his belt.' It was a pistol. There was a lot of Colt .45s around because American servicemen on leave had a habit of losing or selling them.

That moment in the cinema was, he says, when he realised that 'the stoush was dead and good streetfighters were tuppence a ton'. He walked through the darkened cinema to the emergency exit, unbolted the door and went home. By the following Saturday night he had a pistol, too. And the beginning of a reputation that could almost have destroyed him.

LONGLEY is living back in the streets of Ascot Vale where he grew up, within walking distance of the showgrounds where, as a boy, he climbed grandstands at night and caught roosting pigeons to sell to Chinese restaurants. 'Amazing how many pigeons you can fit into your shirt,' he muses.

He is sitting in the living room of the tired cream brick unit he rents. Can't keep a dog because the yard is too small, he says. He loves dogs. One of his favourite books in jail – besides the British commando fitness manual – was about the history and breeding of the English bull mastiff.

Longley had a favourite bull mastiff once, when he lived in Port Melbourne with his then young daughter Lisa and her mother. He says the dog was intelligent and alert and probably saved his life during the dock war.

'The dog kept looking up at the roof as he walked around the back yard. He knew something was wrong. I said to my wife "pack a bag – we're going away for a few days".' The Longleys stayed in a friend's house on the NSW south coast. While they were gone, a next-door neighbour – coincidentally called Bill – had a frightening experience. As he was going through his front gate, his wife called out his name. Immediately, three men with shotguns stood up from behind the parapet on Longley's roof. They were rival painters and dockers, lying in wait for Longley, and had been ready to shoot when they heard the name 'Bill'.

Longley was never without a bull mastiff for years after that. But now, he says, he can't walk a dog enough, though the exercise bike in the hall is helping him get a little fitter. He has always needed exercise to keep his weight down. He has a weakness for strong tea and chocolates.

Family photographs line the walls of his flat and the bookcase is crammed with histories, biographies, dictionaries and a thesaurus. His favourite is Australian correspondent Chester Wilmot's acclaimed war history *The Struggle For Europe*. 'Billy was always the best-read gunman on the docks,' says an erudite friend.

He goes into town to watch a film now and again with his friend and carer, Frances, who lives next door. His favourite film is *On The Waterfront*. Always methodical, he knows what he wants to see next. At the time of writing it was *Downfall*, the European film about Hitler's last days. 'It got five stars in *The Age*,' he says. And television? Twice a week he watches the *The Bill*. Of course. He likes realistic dramas that show flawed characters on both sides of the law.

Longley doesn't rate himself a punter. But he admits he once lost 8000 pounds – then the price of a big house or several small ones – at Canterbury races in the 1960s. He was flying high at the time but soon came back to earth. He reputedly got a share of Australia's then biggest armed robbery in 1970, when three masked men took $587,890 from an armoured van. Twice he thought he was on the way to being a millionaire, he says, but in the end he found out that his mother was right: Crime didn't pay. He lost the money – and 13 years 'buried' in jail while his only daughter grew up and the world passed him by.

Once, he told his brother Reg he dreamed of flying to England, catching the Concorde supersonic airliner to New York and cruising home on the *Queen Mary*. He never did get to leave Australia – but, two years later, his brother the suburban barber did his dream trip: Concorde, ocean liner and all. He tells the story against himself. It is his way of obliquely acknowledging that he took the wrong fork in the path.

His trips out of Melbourne in the past were mostly at night, by road. He and unnamed others would drive to Sydney overnight in time to arrive with the morning traffic, 'do our business' and then leave again in the afternoon peak. It was safer that way. If they had flown, the police and certain well-informed Sydney gangsters would have known as soon as they got off the plane. The consequences could have been fatal.

One of his signature sayings is 'Sydney for money, Melbourne for blokes.' Meaning that you could stay out of sight ('in smoke') in Melbourne because loyal people would protect you, but would immediately be sold out in Sydney. In the underworld version of traditional Melbourne-Sydney rivalry, he says, Sydney crime bosses traditionally imported Melbourne hard men to fight their battles when the going got tough.

Now, he lives with his memories – and a lot of regrets. One is the death of his first wife in a shooting incident of which he was acquitted. Another is that he didn't shoot Jack Twist at Webb Dock back in 1971. Another is that when he was desperate for cash he pawned his grandfather's gold fob watch in the late

1940s. His mother brought it back from Scotland to give to him in 1943 and he would like it more than anything else. It is engraved with his grandfather's name: Lieutenant Commander William Roxburgh.

If anyone out there has it, he'd kill to get it back. Figuratively speaking, of course.

> I always loved Victor and
> I was never going to give
> evidence against him.

9.
COMING CLEAN

SHE was the ace in the pack – the witness that could prove to a jury of strangers how a gang of Melbourne armed robbers became ruthless police killers.

Taskforce detectives had worked on her for months, chipping away, hoping they could turn her against the men they were convinced had ambushed and murdered two young police constables in Walsh Street, South Yarra.

But she knew the rules. To talk to police, let alone give evidence for them, was an act of unforgivable betrayal. In the twisted vernacular of the underworld to give evidence – to tell the truth – is to turn 'dog'. And she was to be the biggest dog of all.

She was to be the 94th – and most important – witness, not only for what she was going to say under oath, but because of whom she was. Experienced defence barristers could easily discredit many of the witnesses in the case.

Career criminals looking to curry favour, men trying to do deals with authorities over their own criminal activities, or those who could provide only small snippets to add to events that took years to build, hours to plan and minutes to execute.

But Wendy Peirce was no outsider looking in. She was the wife of the alleged ringleader and could provide the jury with the chilling details of how and why the gang chose two young policemen they didn't know to ambush and murder in a small street before dawn.

Wendy was no tourist passing through the underworld. Her adult life had been spent in the black and bloody world of Australia's most notorious crime cell – the Pettingill-Allen-Peirce clan, in which violence was seen as a solution and murder an attractive option.

Her husband and the father of her children was Victor George Peirce, the leader of a gang of armed robbers hitting targets around Melbourne.

Wendy Peirce was the reason that police were confident they could convict the men charged with the murders of Steven Tynan and Damian Eyre, who were shot dead on October 12, 1988.

The prosecution case was that Peirce and his crew were driven by a pathological hatred of law enforcement after police killed two of their mates the previous year – Mark Militano in March and Frankie Valastro in June.

Detectives maintained both men, who had long histories of violence, were shot when they refused to surrender and chose to threaten police with guns.

The gang was convinced members of the armed robbery squad had become trigger-happy and embarked on a policy of being judge, jury and executioner. They believed that when frustrated detectives couldn't find the evidence to convict the suspects they would shoot them and later argue the killings were self-defence.

After Militano's death, detectives claim, Peirce and his team began to talk of fighting back. If more of their mates were to be killed by police they would respond by killing two police in return.

There were rumours and whispers of the revenge pact and there was talk that members of the squad could be ambushed in the driveways of their own homes.

Detectives grabbed Victor Peirce, told him they knew he was committing armed robberies and advised him he should pull up while he could.

The stakes were raised and a confrontation of sorts was inevitable.

On October 11, 1988, Peirce's best friend and prolific armed robbery partner, Graeme Jensen, was shot dead by police in a botched arrest at Narre Warren after the suspect went to buy a spark plug for his mower.

It was now flashpoint.

On Wednesday, October 12, a Walsh Street resident reported to police that a white Holden Commodore was apparently abandoned in the street with the bonnet raised, the driver's side door open and the rear passenger side vent window smashed.

At 4.34 am a D24 operator assigned the job to a patrol car using the call sign Prahran 311.

The two young policemen on night patrol in Prahran 311 were too inexperienced to be bored with routine calls and responded immediately.

The driver, Steven Tynan, 22, had been a policeman for two years and nine months. His partner, Damian Eyre, 20, was from a police family and had been in the job for six months after graduating from the academy on April 27, 1988.

It took just seven minutes for the pair to reach the suspect sedan.

Tynan parked the divisional van behind the Holden. Both vehicles were facing north. Eyre got out of the passenger side of the van and walked to the car.

He glanced at the registration sticker on the front window and jotted down the number and expiry date on a sheet of paper on his clipboard.

Meanwhile, his partner went to the open driver's door and slipped behind the wheel.

Eyre then walked around the car and squatted next to Tynan, who was still in the car.

They would have seen that the ignition lock was broken so that the car could be started without a key.

Tynan had started to get out of the car when the shotgun blast hit him. The deadly force threw him back into the car, where he collapsed, with his head between the front bucket seats. It was 4.48 am.

Eyre began to rise from the squatting position when he was shot across his back in the upper left shoulder, also with a shotgun.

It should have been enough to stop anyone dead, but Eyre somehow rose and turned to face his attacker. He grabbed the gunman and fought. Police believe the shotgun discharged twice more, one blast hitting the wall of a Walsh Street house.

Even though he was seriously, but not fatally, wounded, Eyre continued to fight until a second man slipped up next to him and grabbed the policeman's service .38 revolver from its holster, put it to the policeman's head and fired.

Eyre collapsed and was shot again in the back as he lay next to the rear driver's side wheel of the stolen car. He was already dying when the second revolver bullet hit him.

Both Tynan and Eyre died in hospital from massive gunshot wounds without regaining consciousness.

It didn't take detectives long to work out that this was a cold-blooded ambush.

The dumped car had been used as bait to lure police – any police – into the quiet street. At the top of a very short list of suspects was Victor Peirce and his team.

Within a day Victor's mother, Kath Pettingill, the matriarch of the notorious crime family, was quoted saying she knew her children were the prime suspects but denied they were involved.

'It wasn't us,' she said. 'I hate coppers but those boys didn't do anything. Our family wouldn't do that. We were not involved.

'You don't kill two innocent coppers. If you want to get back you would kill the copper who killed Graeme.'

Police responded immediately, conducting a series of sometimes brutal raids. They were sending a clear message to the underworld: all business was off until the police killers were charged and in jail.

But one of the most defiant in the face of constant raids was Wendy Peirce.

Apparently blood loyal to her in-laws, she posed doe-eyed for media with one of her children in debris after her house was raided by heavy-handed police.

Homicide squad detective Jim Conomy formally interviewed her on November 9, 1988.

Not only did she refuse to implicate her husband but she gave him an alibi. They were together all night in a Tullamarine motel and he did not leave.

It was a lie.

On December 30, 1988, Victor Peirce was formally charged with two counts of murder over Walsh Street.

Three other men, Peirce's half-brother Trevor Pettingill, Anthony Farrell and Peter David McEvoy, were charged. Two other suspects, Jedd Houghton and Gary Abdallah, were shot dead by police in separate incidents. Peirce's young nephew Jason Ryan was also charged, although he became a protected witness for the prosecution.

With no witnesses, police built a complex case that relied heavily on forensic evidence linking a shotgun used in Walsh Street to an earlier armed robbery alleged to have been conducted by the suspects, and a series of witnesses who were prepared to swear on oath that the men charged were the killers.

Much of the testimony was tainted by the fact it was from career criminals who were never going to been seen as reliable.

Many had at first denied any knowledge or helped provide alibis for the suspects.

Then, after being subjected to sustained pressure from detectives, they finally agreed to testify.

Members of the Ty-Eyre taskforce set up to investigate the murders continued to visit Wendy Peirce. They didn't use tough-guy tactics but gently tried to persuade her that this would be the one chance she had to change her life – to leave the underworld and make a fresh start. They told her she had reached a fork in the road and had to choose which way she wanted to go.

In July 1989 – eight months after the murders – she would spend three days with Detective Inspector David Sprague and Senior Detective Colin McLaren of the Ty-Eyre taskforce, making an explosive 31-page statement.

On Sunday, July 16, she told the detectives she wished to go into the witness protection scheme. Two days later, in an interview room in homicide she repeated her statement on videotape – a confession that could have condemned her husband to life in prison.

Sporting bleached blonde hair and wearing heavy make-up, she appeared remarkably relaxed as she read her statement. Yes, she had been with her husband at the Tullamarine Motel on the night that Jensen had been killed but 'Victor was absent from the motel most of the night until the morning.'

In other words, he had plenty of time to drive to Walsh Street and return.

She read her statement in a monotone, stumbling over some of the words. But the message was clear. 'He disliked police so much that he would often say to me "I'd love to knock them dogs". His hatred of police was so vicious that at times I was scared to be with him.'

She said the whole family hated police, but Victor was the worst.

'On many occasions he would be holding on to a handgun and would say, "I would love to knock jacks".'

Wendy said there was one armed robbery squad detective 'he wanted to put off'.

In February 1988, after police raided his family, Peirce 'was yelling and screaming and in such a rage from yelling that he started crying from temper,' she said.

Why then had she protected him with a false statement to police?

'I have been an alibi witness for Victor many times. I did so out of loyalty to him and also out of fear. I was well aware he would bash me if I didn't … I was fearful that Victor would kill me if I didn't supply an alibi.'

In this version of events, she said that when Peirce first

learned that Jensen had been killed by police, he had said 'Oh Jesus' and had tears in his eyes.

She told police he then rang McEvoy and said, 'What can we do mate? Graeme's dead, what can we do?'

She said he told her, 'I'm next. They'll shoot me now. They're dogs, they knocked Graeme for no good reason.'

What she then said could have blown a hole in Peirce's story that he spent the night with her.

She said they went to bed with his arm under her head. She heard him get up and get dressed. But she had learned over the previous 13 years when it was best to mind her own business and she chose not to move or call out.

'I heard him leave the motel.' She dozed and when he came back to bed he was cold.

The taskforce was delighted. They had infiltrated the family that lived by the code of silence. Wendy Peirce continued to talk. Tape after tape was recorded that implicated Peirce in murders and unsolved armed robberies.

Police and prosecution lawyers were confident that once a jury heard her version of events they would convict the four men in the dock without hesitation.

After all, why would a woman lie to help convict the father of her children?

For more than a year Wendy Peirce lived in witness protection waiting for the day she would be called to help send her husband to jail.

The committal hearing at the Magistrates' Court proved to be the perfect dress rehearsal. She answered all questions and made it clear her husband was the key figure in the group that killed the two police as a random payback after their mate, Graeme Jensen, had been shot dead by police during an attempted arrest the previous day.

She answered all questions and made it clear her husband was the driving force behind Walsh Street. She was cross-examined ruthlessly but stood up to the examination. A court veteran, she had acted as an unofficial legal assistant during many of the family's battles with the law.

But there were warning signs. In November 1990, shortly after the committal hearing, Wendy Peirce's brother told taskforce joint leader Inspector John Noonan they were about to be ambushed – that she would not give evidence when it counted.

It worried Noonan enough to front Wendy Peirce, who said the claim was 'utter rubbish'.

But it wasn't.

The jury would never hear her testimony. In the pre-trial *voir dire* – closed hearing – at the Supreme Court, Wendy Peirce suddenly changed her story and effectively sabotaged the police case.

After 18 months in witness protection and after swearing to her husband's involvement at the Magistrate's committal hearings, Peirce betrayed her police minders and saved her husband Victor from conviction and a certain lifetime prison sentence.

Not only did she deny that her husband was involved, but she declared that she had never seen him with guns in their Richmond home.

Yet in her earlier police statement she said her husband was an expert at hiding guns and that when she saw him in their shed sawing off the barrel of a shotgun he said to her with the pride of a home handyman, 'This will be a beauty, Witch' ('Witch' was her nickname).

She also knew first hand of her husband's interest in gunplay. She told police that once while sitting with Graeme Jensen,

Victor became annoyed because they had run out of marijuana. 'He was playing with a revolver and said, "Get up and dance".' When she refused, 'he shot twice between my legs' – the bullets were left implanted in the skirting board.

In December 1992, Wendy Peirce was found guilty of perjury and sentenced to a minimum of nine months jail.

In sentencing her, Judge Ross said the perjury was premeditated and she had shown no signs of remorse.

Now, 17 years later, Wendy Peirce has finally admitted what police have always known and no jury would ever hear. Her husband *did* do it.

IT is an early spring afternoon in Port Melbourne where new money, empty nesters and old crooks exist together with feigned indifference towards each other.

Wendy Peirce sits at an outside table near Station Pier, ignoring the bite from the wind off the bay while leafing through a bestselling true crime book.

The other tables outside are empty.

Inside, the café is warm and busy but outside no-one minds if you smoke – and you can chat without worrying about eavesdroppers.

She sees a picture of her husband in the book. A detective is leading him in handcuffs to court. The prisoner's right eye is puffy and closing.

'They bashed him with gun butts,' she says matter-of-factly. 'He needed a few stitches.' She speaks without anger or grief. To her it seems to be just an occupational hazard for the career criminal.

Parked just ten metres away is her husband's 1993 maroon Commodore sedan – the car he was sitting in when he was shot dead in Bay Street, Port Melbourne, on May 1, 2002.

In police circles there is no name more detested than that of Victor Peirce. Many openly rejoiced when he was finally murdered.

When police returned the bloodied sedan after completing forensic testing, Wendy had it cleaned and detailed and decided to keep it 'for sentimental reasons'.

Victor, she explains, had a soft spot for Commodores and almost always used stolen ones when committing armed robberies.

Wendy Peirce has spent nearly 30 years watching, committing and concealing serious crime. She talks of her history with no obvious signs of guilt or embarrassment. What is done is done.

But she has finally agreed to talk, she says, to set the record straight. 'I have been an idiot. If I would have me life back I wouldn't have done this. It has been a total waste.'

She is considering changing her name and trying to bury her past. She says her son Victor junior is burdened with carrying the name of his father, a brutal gunman, drug dealer, police killer and gangland murder victim.

Her daughter is still filled with anguish at losing her father to an underworld ambush. Her youngest son goes to school near where his father was shot dead.

So why did she agree to give evidence for the police and then change her mind before the trial?

Peirce says she was never going to give evidence. That her decision to go into witness protection was part of a long-range family plan to sabotage the prosecution from the inside.

She now says that although he organised the murders, her husband felt there would never be enough evidence to justify his arrest. 'He covered his tracks and he didn't think he'd get pinched,' she says.

But when Victor Peirce's sister, Vicki Brooks, and her son Jason Ryan, went into witness protection, the police case became stronger.

At first Wendy Peirce stayed staunch, following the underworld code of refusing to make admissions. 'My first statement was to Jim Conomy (on November 9) stating that we had nothing to do with it. Noonan wanted to charge me with murder.'

Wendy Peirce claims she knew her alibi was worthless and no-one would believe her. She claims that Peter Allen – Victor's half-brother and the jailhouse lawyer of the family – was the one who decided Wendy would be more valuable if she appeared to change sides.

'He said, "If you give evidence for Victor he'll go down (be convicted). With your priors (convictions) the jury won't believe you".'

'He said that if I somersaulted them (changed sides) ... Peter said I would get no more than 18 months for perjury and he was spot on.'

She said she never intended to give evidence against Victor and that she stayed in contact with him even when in witness protection.

'I would talk to mum and Kath (Pettingill, Victor's mother) was there to pass on messages to Victor. I was posting him letters and photos. I always loved Victor and I was never going to give evidence against him.'

Police claim the suggestion that Wendy was planted as a witness is a fantasy.

One member of the taskforce says she saw the chance to start a new life and grabbed it but had second thoughts when she realised that she would have to work rather than living off the proceeds of drugs and armed robberies.

Another said she was happy when she was duchessed by the taskforce but felt miffed when moved to Canberra and put in public housing by witness protection.

'She saw that even before the trial she was no longer special. She realised that after she had given evidence she would be left to fend for herself,' one policeman said.

One detective said she was besotted by one of her guards and decided to flip sides and return to the Peirce camp when the policeman was moved to other duties.

Inspector John Noonan, who was joint head of the taskforce, blames the legal system. It was simply too long from arrest to the trial to hold the unreliable Peirce.

He says he has no doubt if a jury had heard her evidence, all four accused men would have been convicted.

'They (Victor Peirce and his family) kept at her. Getting messages to her that everything would be all right and if she changed her story back she would move back with Victor. She was getting messages from Peirce in prison through third parties that he understood the pressure she was under, but they belonged together.'

'They told her they could look after her better than the police.'

The treatment of Wendy Peirce split the taskforce when some members were banned from dealing with her for fear their confrontational style would push her out of the prosecution camp.

Joint-taskforce head, Commander David Sprague, said police lacked the professionalism in witness protection at the time to deal with someone like Wendy Peirce.

'She could not cope with witness protection. I think we had a real chance in the early days but as the case dragged on she changed sides again.'

He said she was difficult to control, continuing to shoplift and drive without a licence while under witness protection.

In the early months, she was protected by the taskforce and treated as a star. She stayed in hotels – some of them luxurious – and was constantly moved.

She was flattered, taken out for meals and her children entertained with outings that included sailing trips around Port Phillip Bay.

But as the months dragged on towards the trial, she was put into the much less glamorous witness protection program.

Many of her young guards had trouble concealing their contempt for the wife of a police killer. She had lost her friends and her extended dysfunctional family and the detectives who had persuaded her to become a prosecution witness were no longer there to fortify her weakening resolve.

Senior police say she had a glimpse of her future as a struggling single mother. And she didn't like it.

WENDY Peirce says her husband was a criminal with two great passions – his love of armed robberies and his hatred of police. 'Victor was the planner. He loved doing stick-ups. He was the one who would do all the planning and tell the others what to do.'

Police say the core members in the team, known as the Flemington Crew, were Jedd Houghton, Graeme Jensen, Peter David McEvoy, Paul Prideaux and Lindsay Rountree. The specialist car thief for the gang was Gary Abdallah.

Jedd Houghton would be shot dead by police in a Bendigo caravan park on November 17, 1988. Abdallah was shot dead by police in a Carlton flat on April, 1989.

'He (Abdallah) was always good with Holdens. Victor would tell him to steal two and have one left at a certain spot.' The armed robbery team would do the job in one stolen Holden before swapping to the second a few kilometres away.

To Peirce it was a job. Nearly every work-day he would head off to observe possible targets and plan armed robberies. 'He was an absolute expert,' she says proudly.

But if it was a job, he certainly loved his work.

'He told me he often got an erection when he charged into a bank. He was just so excited. He planned the jobs and then they did the robberies. He loved doing banks – he just loved it. He got off on it.

'I always got him to ring me straight after a job to make sure he was okay. Then I'd tell him to get home with the money. I loved it.'

The most money she saw was $200,000 after Peirce robbed the ANZ bank in Ringwood in January, 1988. 'He did heaps, he did over twenty armed robberies.'

The money, she now admits, was laundered through lawyer Tom Scriva, but none remains.

'We wasted it all. We wanted to buy a new house near Diggers Rest. We had five acres picked out but we just spent all the money.'

Gaetano 'Tom' Scriva, 55, died of natural causes in July 2000 but by then much of the black money he was holding for his gangster clients had disappeared.

Scriva's father Michele was a Melbourne mafia figure connected with the wholesale fruit and vegetable market. In 1945, Scriva senior was acquitted of the murder of Giuseppe 'Fat Joe' Versace in what was probably Victoria's first mafia hit. Versace was stabbed 91 times.

Michele Scriva was later sentenced to hang for stabbing Frederick Duffy to death in North Melbourne, but the sentence was later commuted and he served 10 years.

Scriva was a trusted lieutenant to Godfather Liborio Benvenuto, who died of natural causes in 1988. Much later, Benvenuto's son Frank would become good friends with Peirce.

According to Wendy, her husband robbed banks in East Bentleigh, Ringwood and Knox City in 1988. He also hit security guards carrying cash boxes into banks and attacked couriers who were picking up large amounts of cash.

'He would knock them out and take the money,' she recalls.

She says that when armed robbery squad detectives came to interview him, he told her 'if he didn't come back they had loaded him (fabricated evidence to justify an arrest). He came home and said they told him to pull up on the banks or they would load him'.

She confirms the stick-up crew saw the armed robbery squad as its enemy and believed the detectives were methodically murdering criminals they could not convict.

The pact to kill two police for every armed robber? 'It was more Jedd and Macca (McEvoy) than the others.'

'Jedd was the trigger man; he had the shotgun. Macca took the (Damian Eyre's) handgun. Victor was pissed off with him for that. Abdallah knocked (stole) the car. I don't think (Anthony) Farrell and Trevor (Pettingill) were even there.'

Wendy Peirce says Victor was convinced police were going to kill him. 'We went on the run, living in motels with the kids.

'It (Walsh Street) was spur of the moment. We were on the run. Victor was the organiser.'

But she says he showed no regrets over what he did. 'He just said, "They deserved their whack. It could have been me".'

According to Wendy, Jensen's violent death hit Peirce hard. 'Graeme was his best mate. He idolised him.'

But what Peirce didn't know at the time was that his best mate and his wife were having an affair. 'It just happened. Graeme would come over to see Victor to talk about jobs and he would wink at me. Then he came over and Victor wasn't there and it just happened.'

It was the relationship rather than the double murder that led Peirce to his only moment of remorse.

He told her, 'If I had known about the affair I wouldn't have done it (Walsh Street).'

IT has taken Wendy Peirce almost two years – since agents acting for the Underbelly Conglomerate first approached her – to finally agree to tell her story.

She has been interviewed on the record and then later asked for her story to remain unpublished. Now she says she is ready to tell the truth.

Her private life is a disaster, her family is collapsing and she is heavily in debt.

She says she hopes her life can show others that there is no glamour in the underworld. She claims that the death of her husband has finally given her the victim's perspective of crime.

She was just a teenager from a law-abiding family when she met Victor Peirce and his mother, Kath Pettingill. She fell in love both with the criminal and his gangster lifestyle.

But in 1983 she says Victor wanted to leave his criminal past and get a job.

He had just been released from Ararat prison after serving two years and they moved into a rented unit in Albert Park, suburbs away from the rest of his criminal family.

But Peirce's half-brother, the notorious Dennis Allen, offered to give them a house next to his, in Chestnut Street, Richmond.

'Once we moved in, that was the end. Victor was always helping out Dennis. If we hadn't moved there, then none of this would have happened – none of the murders, the armed robberies and the drugs. If we hadn't moved there, then Victor would be alive today and so would those two police (Tynan and Eyre).'

Allen was a prolific drug dealer in the early 1980s. 'I saw Victor with cash, sometimes $50,000, sometimes $100,000. I saw Dennis with $500,000.'

Allen had many bank accounts but also liked to bury cash so it could never be traced. Much of it was never recovered when he died of natural causes in 1987. 'When he got sick, he couldn't remember anything. It must all still be buried around Richmond.'

Police say Allen was responsible for up to 11 murders and Wendy says she learned from experience to read the signs when her brother-in-law 'was about to go off'.

One day in August 1984 she saw him turn and look coldly at small-time crook Wayne Stanhope, then turn up the volume of the stereo – not because he loved music but to drown the shots he was about to fire.

'I told him, "Not in my house".' Allen grudgingly agreed and took Stanhope next door to shoot him, but left the body in the boot of a car in the street for two days.

Wendy Peirce later took police to a bush area near Ballan where Stanhope was buried. Detectives found the burnt-out car but could not find the body although they remain convinced they were close.

Allen was blamed for the deaths of Victor Gouroff and Greg Pasche in 1983, Helga Wagnegg in 1984 and Anton Kenny in 1985.

'Dennis gave Helga Wagnegg pure heroin. They poured buckets of water from the Yarra River down her throat to try to make it look like she drowned.

'Anton did nothing wrong. There was no reason. Dennis didn't need a reason.

'Victor Gouroff killed Greg Pasche. Dennis killed Gouroff because he didn't get rid of the body properly.

'Pasche said something out of school and Gouroff stabbed him. He was in the kitchen saying, "Dennis, help me, help me". Dennis picked up a bayonet and stabbed him in the head. They dragged him into the backyard and wrapped him up. There was no need for any of this. It was madness.'

After the Walsh Street trial, many police expected Wendy Peirce to eventually to be murdered by her husband or one of his criminal associates – but they remained together, when he was out of jail.

In 2001 Peirce's best friend Frank Benvenuto was murdered – almost certainly by Andrew 'Benji' Veniamin, who was shot dead in a Carlton restaurant in 2004.

She says Benvenuto was murdered because he had ordered the killing of another market identity in the 1990s.

When Benvenuto lay dying, he managed to ring Victor on his mobile phone. 'He just groaned.'

A few minutes later, the phone rang again. It was a major crime figure informing Peirce that Benvenuto was dead. How he knew so quickly has never been explained. 'There was $64,000 in the boot of Frank's car and they didn't even take it,' she said.

'Benji wanted a meeting with Victor and they met in a Port Melbourne park. He wanted to know if Victor was going to back up for Frank. He was his best mate. Victor took a gun and Benji would have been armed.'

They agreed there would be no payback.

'Frank kept my family going for six years (While Victor was in jail). Frank was a lovely man.'

Wendy Peirce says she has no regrets about refusing to implicate her husband at the Walsh St trial even though it condemned her to bring up her children in the criminal world. 'I loved Victor – I can't change that.'

She used to hate police but seeing them professionally investigate her husband's death – even though he had killed two of theirs – made her think again.

She has told her story, she says, to free herself from the past and so no one can accuse her of hiding from what she has done. She says her children have suffered because of the choices she made and she now regrets wasting her life in the world of violence, drugs and treachery.

'I can't take back what I have done but it is all worth nothing. If I say sorry most people won't believe me. I just don't want my children to suffer because of what we did.'

Wendy Peirce has been a central figure in violent crime for nearly 30 years but only after seeing the lasting anguish of her children following the murder of their father has she finally understood how victims suffer.

'I want to keep away from criminals now. I want to bring my kids up in peace. I am proud of my children. They have not become involved in criminal activities. I wish I could be like them.'

> This would just be another
> burden to the man who had
> always put himself first.

10.
MUMMY'S BOY

JOHN Myles Sharpe appeared to be just another family man doing the best he could to raise a family and get ahead. Not a born risk-taker, he had finally quit his safe but boring job with a bank and had ventured out of his comfort zone into a business he hoped eventually to own. Married with a daughter and another child on the way, he was the sort of everyman we pass on the street every day.

But John Myles Sharpe was different, although no-one knew it back then. Underneath that mild exterior was a cold-blooded monster.

We are supposed to be able to sense evil. Violent people tend to have a threatening presence or a chequered history. Most of us leave footprints that lead to the present but there was nothing much about Sharpe to indicate the man he would become. It would take 37 years for the true John Sharpe to surface, leaving even experienced homicide detectives wondering about their neighbours. Nothing stood out in his past as an event that might twist his character.

Sharpe's background was as plain as it was stable. He was the fifth of six children born to a shop-keeping couple who lived in the Melbourne seaside suburb of Mornington. In his lifetime he never ventured far from home … except perhaps in his head.

Although he was the fifth child he was the family's first son and many saw him as a little spoilt, needy and inclined to be a mummy's boy. He had a habit of whining when things didn't go his way but those who knew the family hoped that age would round out his character. Schooled locally, the unremarkable student would become the equally unremarkable adult. A grey man in a world filled with colour. A life in sepia.

He plugged on in school, without the dash to be a personality and without the brains to be a nerd, before he failed year 12 in 1984. He then moved seamlessly to the white-collar safety net of a job with the State Bank.

When the bank was taken over by the Commonwealth Bank and many of his colleagues took redundancies and moved on, Sharpe just kept his head down and plodded on. It was in this job that the grey man with the dull life finally met someone with the energy and ambition he lacked – New Zealand-born Anna Marie Kemp.

Unlike Sharpe, who lived his life within minutes of his childhood home, Anna was prepared to move to improve hers. At the age of 27 she left New Zealand with her close friend, Jenny Young, and moved to the bayside suburb of Mentone. She almost immediately applied for a job with the Commonwealth Bank and, with her cheery personality and obvious people skills, was employed as a customer service operator. She was appointed to her local branch at Mentone, where the quiet and shy Sharpe was already working. Despite him being five years younger and lacking the sense of fun of the New Zealander, they began to date and were married on October 30, 1994.

Many of Anna Kemp's friends could not see the attraction. Some of his few friends also wondered what she could see in the socially inept bank worker. Those who knew them said they were virtually opposites. She was strong-willed, direct, open, bubbly and had a wicked sense of humour. He was passive, quiet, manipulative and cunning. She enjoyed meeting people, while he was socially awkward. And even though he was an adult, he still tended to run to mummy when things didn't work out. Perhaps his attraction to the slightly older, much stronger and more purposeful Anna was the replacement of one dominant woman with another. He didn't marry her to share his life but to fix it.

Anna resigned from the bank and tried her hand in other business. He just stayed where he was. She became an Australian citizen on June 19, 2001, while he was treading water. Finally, and largely due to the encouragement of his wife, Sharpe left the bank in August 2002 to strike out of his comfort zone. He became a partner in a conveyancing business – Fast Trak Conveyancing – and hoped to eventually take over the business when the older man retired. His last day at the bank after seventeen years was the same day his wife gave birth to their first child, Gracie Louise. It was Friday, August 13. Black Friday.

SHARPE struggled with any form of change and was definitely not the man for a crisis. Gracie's birth was not easy. She was delivered by emergency caesarean at The Bays Hospital in

Mornington. When her parents learned the baby was born with a congenital abnormality in her hips, the cold and distant father simply withdrew further. It was Anna who had to cope and for the new mother it would be a major struggle. The infant underwent orthopaedic treatment and had to wear a corrective harness for her first three months. The unsettled and uncomfortable Gracie was a sporadic feeder and a spasmodic sleeper. If Anna had not known before, she now realised there were two babies in the house – her daughter and her spoilt husband. She knew she needed help but realised that it would not come from John.

In November, three months after the birth, she went to the Hillview Maternity Unit of Peninsula Health and confided to medical staff that she was anxious and struggling to cope. Three times she and Gracie were admitted for respite to try to establish regular sleeping and eating patterns. But instead of showing real concern and compassion for Anna and Gracie, Sharpe began to head home to his mother where he complained that his wife was 'moody and bossy'.

After the corrective harness was removed, Gracie quickly settled down – unlike her father. She was enrolled at a Mornington childcare centre where staff described her as 'a gorgeous little girl with a smile on her face ... a delight to look after'.

With only one income – as with many young families – money was tight, so they decided to sell their home and move to a smaller one. But Sharpe would not abandon the area where he had lived all his life and they moved from Spinnaker Rise to a two-bedroom, double-storey weatherboard in Prince Street – less than two kilometres from his parents' home.

Although the house was smaller, Anna saw it as an opportunity. It was just two streets to the beach and she already had plans to renovate. They bought the house in September 2003 and two months later she announced she was pregnant again. Rather than show excitement at the news, Sharpe brooded again. He would later say that their sex life was so limited he was surprised she was expecting.

The first child had been difficult enough and their marriage was under strain. This would just be another burden to the man who had always put himself first. In January 2004, Anna went to an obstetrician, Dr Andrew Griffiths, who confirmed she was eleven weeks pregnant.

She told him the pregnancy was unplanned. She then added that there was a 'lack of enthusiasm' from her husband at the news they were to have a second baby. John Sharpe the mild-mannered but mean-spirited former bank worker was beginning to feel trapped – and it was then that he began to plan his dreadful escape.

DESPITE living close to Port Phillip Bay all his life, Sharpe was not one for seaside activities so it would have come as a surprise to those who knew him that he chose to wander into Sport Phillip Marine in Main Street, Mornington, to buy a high-powered spear gun. That is, it would have been a surprise if he had told anyone, but he chose to keep his purchase to himself. Spear fishers usually only carry one spear. They fire, retrieve and then fire again.

But when Sharpe bought his new black spear gun he insisted on buying a second stainless steel spear to go with the one already included. The former bank employee chose to pay cash, knowing that a credit card would leave a record of his $190 purchase – a record that no doubt would have led his wife to ask why he had decided to take up spear fishing as a hobby.

Or perhaps he was concerned about who else would be

interested if at some time in the future his financial records were to be examined as part of a criminal investigation.

Some time after he bought the gun – from a shop only a few doors from the local police station – he decided to test it. Not in the bay just a few minutes away but secretly, in the backyard of the Spinnaker Rise home. It worked perfectly.

On March 3, the Sharpes moved to their new smaller home. Boxes were unpacked, cupboards filled and furniture shifted. But John Sharpe made sure no-one saw him carry and hide his secret purchase on the floor in the corner of the garage. Sharpe rang a local tradesman and organised a time to have a new television antenna fitted and electric cables checked. The appointment was for 9am on Wednesday, March 24.

Shortly after moving in, Anna began to make contact with her friends to visit the new home. The first was her fellow New Zealander Jenny Young, who came to dinner on the night of Friday, March 19, and stayed the night – sleeping on a fold-up sofa bed in the lounge room that was already made up. Anna told her that Sharpe sometimes slept in the bed. Jenny thought nothing of it, as it was not unusual for the parents of a baby occasionally to sleep apart.

The next day Anna and her old friend went to lunch. They chatted but there was no talk of marriage problems. Young thought her friend looked relaxed and happy. She would never see Anna again.

When the Sharpes were photographed on Sunday, March 21, it looked like a snapshot of a happy family. The parents and their little girl took a steam-train ride from Mornington to Moorooduc for the birthday of Sharpe's nephew.

The truth was that many members of the Sharpe family were drawn to Anna – a relative by marriage – rather than to John, who was one of their own. She was open, friendly and interested in others. John was withdrawn and seemingly only interested in himself. He was tolerated while she was truly liked. The needy Sharpe's social life centred on his family while Anna had built a strong group of her own friends. She enjoyed some, but not all, family functions while his life tended to revolve around them.

The fact that she would not always fall in with him was a source of continued irritation. But this day there seemed no conflict and family members at the barbecue in the park remember Anna as happy and excited about her plans with the house. Gracie was seen laughing and playing with her young cousins. Even Sharpe appeared to enjoy himself – as much as he ever could. The distant parent even seemed to indulge in quality time, taking his only daughter for a stroll around the local lake.

But the image of the perfect extended family was a lie. The Sharpes had argued and bickered about John's refusal to stand up on his own and his continued emotional reliance on his parents. He would tell police much later he had to pretend Anna was sick when she refused to attend some family functions.

'You know, there's many times she would just say, "I'm never, never going to a family thing again", or "I'm never going to their house again".' Even while he went for the walk with his little girl, Sharpe knew he would soon be a murderer. It was only a matter of time.

ON Monday, March 22, at 9am Anna took Gracie to childcare as usual and picked her up three hours later. That morning she rang her mother, Lilia Gebler, in New Zealand. During the hour-long chat she complained of feeling a little unwell but brightened when she spoke of the alterations she planned for the family home. Already they had replaced old-fashioned lights with down-lights and removed blinds from the sunroom to fill the house with natural light.

That afternoon a close friend and former workmate named Samantha Jeffrey called Anna. She later told police that Anna sounded upbeat and they arranged to meet on Friday so Samantha could see the new home. Anna wrote a quick note on the calendar to remind her of the meeting. That night another friend rang. They talked about her pregnancy and the family picnic. They agreed to catch up during Easter.

While Anna was annoyed by her husband's lethargy, she remained positive and was already preparing for the birth of their second child.

The next day she rang her private health insurance fund to ask when she should add her unborn child to the family cover. She said she would ring back after the birth.

Telling what happened next relies on a version of events provided to police by John Sharpe who, since he was a child, manipulated the truth to place himself in the best light. But there was nothing he could say that could alter the unspeakable facts.

According to Sharpe, who was now working from home, he and his wife argued and bickered during that Tuesday. He told police he could not remember what started the dispute, but that in itself was not unusual, as they were always arguing. They went to bed just before 10pm and while his wife slept he lay awake thinking about how unhappy his marriage and his life had turned out to be.

He hated the fact that he was so easily dominated and lacked the strength of character to change. 'She was very strong. Like, the one that would, if you like, wear the pants in the family ... it seemed to be so very much sort of "her way or the highway" ... It was almost like it was her house and I was living in it, sort of thing, but, you know, that type of thing,' Sharpe would tell police in his attempts to explain the unspeakable.

He got out of bed, went to the garage, grabbed the spear gun, loaded it and crept back into the bedroom.

He knelt on the bed over his wife, placed the spear against her left temple and fired. Anna's breathing began to shudder but instead of stopping, just continued. Sharpe reloaded and fired again into the temple.

This time her breathing appeared to stop. He covered her with towels, closed the bedroom door, went downstairs and then went to sleep on the sofa bed as his little daughter slept in a nearby bedroom. The following day he woke about 7am and fed and changed Gracie before taking her to childcare. It was business as usual.

Sharpe appeared calm when, as arranged, a tradesman from Jim's Antennas arrived that morning. Sharpe informed the worker he couldn't go upstairs, as his wife was sick in bed. He paid by credit card and the tradesman left around 11am. Soon after, around 11.30, another friend of Anna's rang and left a message on the answering machine asking what time on Saturday should she pop around to have a look at the new house. Sharpe returned to the childcare centre to collect his daughter. Staff said that day was the first time the father had dropped off or collected Gracie.

While his daughter slept and played inside, he dug a shallow grave in the backyard. Between 6 and 7pm he took a blue plastic tarpaulin upstairs, nudged his wife and, once satisfied she was dead, tried to remove the spears only to find they would not move. He then rotated the shafts leaving the heads in his wife's skull.

He dragged her in the sheets onto the tarpaulin, then downstairs and buried her in the pre-dug grave. He began to prepare a story that she had left him and Gracie for another man – she was having an affair, that the unborn child was not his and she had left in a 'silvery coloured car'.

For the next few weeks, Sharpe slowly disposed of Anna's clothing and personal belongings in the Mornington tip transfer station. He would get a local rubbish remover to take items, including the marital mattress, for disposal. He bought a new queen-size mattress from a local furniture store. The banker, with knowledge of money trails, paid cash to try to stop police tracing the purchase.

On the Thursday, he rang the childcare centre to tell staff Gracie was ill and would not be attending. That afternoon he started to ring his wife's closest friends, tearfully telling them that Anna had left him and he was going to put Gracie in full-time childcare.

He took Gracie to the centre the following day but when he collected her he told staff he had separated from his wife and this would be the last day his daughter would be attending. He asked for his final account to be sent home. The last time staff saw Gracie was walking out of the centre, holding her father's hand.

The pressure was building on Sharpe. There were three messages from New Zealand from Anna's mother – first social, then increasingly anxious, pleading for a return phone call. Sharpe rang back that night telling the incredulous mother that Anna had left him for another man.

She told him she found the story hard to believe. He said he would ring back the next day to explain further.

As promised, he rang saying Anna had left him and was returning the next day to collect Gracie. Anna's brother, Gerald, then rang Sharpe and said that if his sister did not ring him, he would take the matter to the police.

Sharpe immediately responded that he had to look after Gracie and abruptly hung up.

On the Sunday he rang Anna's mother to say that Gracie was now gone. But it was how he delivered the news that convinced Anna's mother to call the police. He said, 'Gracie belongs with her mother. She is now in a bigger and better place.'

Forty minutes later, she rang back and left a short message. She was going to the police.

DOMESTIC murders are the stock-in-trade of the homicide squad. While no murder is routine and every case a tragedy, the 'domestic' is usually the easiest to understand and the easiest to solve. But detectives who thought they had seen the worst of the human spirit had to think again as the Sharpe case was slowly pieced together.

It will never be known when John Sharpe decided that to sustain his story that his wife had left him, his young daughter had to die, too. Some say he must have considered it an option when, more than a month earlier, he bought the spear gun and insisted on buying a second spear. Others think he was so self-centred that once he saw his story had to be strengthened, the idea of sacrificing his own child to save himself came easily.

Certainly, even in his self-serving confession, he could not tell police when he decided to kill Gracie. But he said from the moment he killed his wife he started to have thoughts of killing his daughter.

He would tell police that in the days after he killed his wife he returned to the same local marine shop to buy another spear. And the man with no apparent conscience took his trusting little girl with him.

In his formal record of interview he would be asked by Detective Sergeant Shane Brundell, of the homicide squad missing person's unit, 'Was Gracie with you at the time that you bought it?

Sharpe responded, 'She was'.

Brundell asked, 'And what was your intention when buying that spear?'

Sharpe replied, 'That it was going to be used – or most likely would have to be used on Gracie to try and make this bullshit I was trying to make out work.'

Sharpe knew there would be a need for sedation to dull the pain. Not for his little victim but for himself. He drank several glasses of scotch and coke before he killed his daughter while she slept, using the spear gun. There is no need to publish details of the murder. Sharpe can take them to his grave.

But the man who killed his wife, his unborn child and his daughter would spend the next three months building a straw house of lies. What he didn't know was that for much of the time police were watching and each layer of deceit would compound his guilt. He was effectively building the case against himself. He disposed of his daughter's body in a hard waste collection bin and over the next week dumped her cot, clothes and toys to give the appearance they had been taken by her mother.

Once he knew police would be investigating the disappearances, he began to try to leave an electronic trail that they would invariably find to indicate his wife had simply walked out with Gracie. Just hours after he killed his daughter, he used Anna's mobile phone to ring home. In the next two months he would use the phone a further seven times to try to lead police to believe she was still alive. He would spread a story that she had moved to Chelsea with her new lover. To help support the black fairytale, he used her Visa card to make five withdrawals over two months from a Chelsea ATM.

On March 29, he used the home computer to send a fake email from Anna to her brother saying she needed space and had fallen in love with another man who was the father of her unborn child. Sharpe rang her brother Gerald to say Anna had collected Gracie two days earlier. He asked if anyone had been to the police, suggesting it would be counterproductive as Anna wanted space.

He said he feared that if police became involved the delicate situation could get worse. He said he wanted Anna to have a chance to think and was concerned that any further complications could result in difficulties for him having access to Gracie. But he was hours too late. Earlier that day Anna's mother had gone to a Dunedin police constable to say her daughter and grandchild were missing and she feared for their safety. Sharpe kept trying to stay ahead of the posse he knew must surely soon be on its way.

With the body of his wife in a freshly-dug grave in the backyard he was only one police visit away from discovery. So he headed to his local Bunnings hardware store and bought a roll of duct tape, two tarpaulins and a Homelite brand 1800-watt electric chainsaw. He paid cash.

He returned a call from a New Zealand detective, Senior Sergeant Phil Foster, and again claimed his wife needed 'space'. Sharpe gave Foster Anna's mobile number. Foster rang the number, leaving a message that Anna should ring her worried mother.

Sharpe exhumed the body and used the chainsaw to cut it into three pieces. He wrapped the remains and disposed of them at the local hard waste bins at the Mornington transfer station. He dumped the chainsaw and other incriminating items in local refuse bins. He typed letters and emails to Anna's friends and family with a consistent message: 'Yes, I am fine but give me space'. One of the friends who received a letter knew the wording was just not Anna and became increasingly suspicious.

On May 1, Sharpe went to the Frankston Library and used the computer to order flowers through Interflora to be sent to Anna's mother. He paid with Anna's credit card. The flowers arrived with a message: 'For Mothers Day and your birthday in one hit. I'll be thinking of you on both days and sending my love. My freedom is precious – I hope you understand. Love Anna'.

The mother understood, all right. She understood there was no way her daughter had sent the flowers. With every attempted cover-up, Sharpe was convincing those around him that he was a double murderer. Some members of his own family would start to see the truth but there were others who would stick by him blindly – making the police investigation more difficult and drawing out the agony for months.

On May 20 New Zealand police contacted the Victoria Police homicide missing persons unit. The situation was no longer to be treated as a messy domestic dispute. It was a likely double murder. That night police went to Sharpe's house and he was taken to the Mornington police station where he provided his well-rehearsed story. He said Anna had been home many times to pick up personal items for her and Gracie. He even provided a written statement for police on what had happened over the past two months. Like him, it was weak, shallow and unbelievable – so much so that detectives decided to watch the man who claimed his wife had walked out on him. The following day police launched a surveillance operation on Sharpe. On that first morning he was seen hiding a plastic bag near a toilet block at Mornington. It contained Anna's mobile phone and her Visa card.

Police followed Sharpe as he went to a series of beachside

bins, dumping evidence that was immediately retrieved and added to other damning pieces in the puzzle. Items collected included Anna's driver's licence, an invoice from the rubbish man who collected the bloodied double-bed mattress and handwritten notes on his version of the disappearance of his wife and child. In another bin police found more handwritten notes, this time outlining a story that he had seized Anna's mobile phone and cards when she came to collect Gracie in a desperate attempt to make her come home.

He would later admit to detectives that these were 'cheat notes' he made when rehearsing a back-up story he would give to police if he were to be confronted with the evidence. The pressure was mounting. He reverted to type, scuttling home to his parents.

The media repeatedly interviewed him but no-one believed his story. He told one reporter: 'I understand people will have their own opinions, but I can't do anything to change what people think. I also understand that the police have a job to do and obviously they have to investigate me and question me. I've been fully cooperative with the police and I will continue to be.'

He said he was hurt by suggestions he was cold-hearted. 'The things you do as a husband and a father and the effort you put in … (then) getting painted that you don't care about your daughter and marriage … it's soul-destroying.' Police interviewed him on June 10 at Mornington but again he stuck to his story.

While police made it clear they believed Anna and Gracie were dead, Sharpe tried to maintain his public charade. Flanked by his parents and holding a picture of his daughter he read a statement in his quavering voice, 'Anna, our marriage may be over but I still love you and you are the mother of our beautiful

daughter Gracie, whom we both adore more than anyone else. I
know the current circumstances are very stressful for you and
everyone concerned, including all our families, and that we are
very private people. We need to resolve this. My biggest fear is
being denied a part of Gracie's future.' Later he would say, 'I
just want to see my daughter'.

HOMICIDE interviews are usually understated affairs. The
trained detective asks hundreds and sometimes thousands of
questions, playing a game of chess with suspects. It is not a
grilling. The truth is more often teased out of the suspects than
forced out. People can be caught lying, but that alone won't
crack a case. They can lie out of fear, to cover up embarrassment or because they are just born liars. That does not mean
they are necessarily killers. The questions often seem irrelevant
but they are asked with an eye to a jury. They need the suspect
to make admissions that can corroborate a crime – to reveal
facts that only the killer could know. A confession – 'I did it' –
is never enough.

So when police were finally ready to confront Sharpe they
had to remain calm and non-judgmental. He was a weak man
likely to freeze at the first stern word. Intimidated people clam
up. No matter what he said, the detectives – mostly men with
wives and children – could not betray the horror at what he
would say and their contempt for what he had become. While
they had already decided to charge him with the murders, the
interview would be pivotal because the case was largely
circumstantial. Without a confession, police would have had to
go to court without the bodies of the pregnant woman and the
little girl, killed months earlier.

It was 9.31am on June 22 when Senior Detective Mark
Kennedy asked the first question of Sharpe in the homicide

interview. Sharpe responded to any questions he thought were difficult with the standard, 'On legal advice, I won't answer the question'.

Sharpe's story was clearly bogus but after more than 200 questions he was sticking to it. At question 219 Kennedy asked, 'Is there anything else that you have not told us in relation to the disappearances of Anna and Gracie?' He declined to answer. Then police pumped up the pressure. They showed him pictures of the beaches and bins where they had found items he had dumped. They showed him the mobile phone and cards they had recovered. Then, making sure he was comfortable, they played him a short video. It was of Sharpe, sneaking around the toilet block to where he had hidden Anna's phone and cards in a plastic bag. Kennedy asked, 'I put it to you John, that that was actually you in that video, have you any comment to make in relation to that?'

They showed him items from the house that he had tried to dump, and which police had found. Books including one called *Up The Duff* aimed at women who are pregnant and another containing 50,000 names for babies. It was from this book that Anna had planned to find the name for her unborn son. After two hours and 378 questions the interview was suspended – but just for 25 minutes. John Sharpe was then formally charged with the two murders. At 12.16 the interview ended.

Rather than taking Sharpe directly to court, the investigating team allowed him to see members of his family. This was not an act of compassion but an attempt to persuade him to open up. There were the mandatory tears and hugs before he finally confessed to the detectives outside the interview room that he killed his wife and daughter. But that was not enough. They needed it on videotape. So, two hours later, he returned to the interview room and in answer to a question from Detective

Sergeant Shane Brundell, Sharpe finally said what police had known for weeks: 'Well, that I did have ... well, that I had killed Anna and also Gracie.'

This time he answered questions and apologised when he couldn't remember little details. He seemed to treat Detective Sergeant Brundell as a new-found friend, referring to him as Shane during the questioning. Finally, on question 1366, asked if he understood that he had been charged with the murders, Sharpe answered, 'I do, Shane.'

It should have been the end of the investigation but police had to find the remains. For nearly three weeks they searched through a one metre deep, 60 square metre area at the Mornington landfill site before they found what was left of the bodies.

On August 5, 2005, Supreme Court Justice Bernard Bongiorno sentenced Sharpe for the double murder. In his sentencing remarks Bongiorno, a former Director of Public Prosecutions, said: *From the moment you killed your wife you began to have thoughts that you would have to kill Gracie to maintain your façade of innocence with respect to Anna's murder. Indeed, at some time between your wife's death and the time you actually killed your daughter, you took her with you to Sport Phillip Marine whilst you purchased another spear for the spear gun. There could have been only one reason for that purchase, which was carried out in circumstances of unspeakable callousness.*

The judge said that according to a forensic psychiatrist who examined Sharpe, he was *socially inept, dependant, passive and a retiring individual.* Another psychiatrist ... *considered you to be an inadequate, isolated and withdrawn individual. You had few appropriate social skills and few friends. He thought you were very dependant on your parents and lacked the psychological resources to cope with the stressors in your life.*

Bongiorno said Sharpe had planned Anna's death: *Your killing your wife was no impulsive act of desperation.* He described the murder as ... *singular in its barbarity ... (and) there was the fact that your wife was pregnant. Your act effectively destroyed two lives, not one.* Of the murder of Sharpe's daughter, the judge said: *Gracie was a defenceless child for whom you had a legal and, more importantly, a moral responsibility.*

In sentencing Sharpe to life with a minimum of 33 years' jail, Bongiorno said he doubted the double murderer was truly sorry for what he had done. *You may reach a state of genuine remorse; it is to be hoped that you do. A positive finding that you have done so yet, however, cannot be made. Finally, your time in prison, especially in the early years of your sentence, is likely to be marked by hostility and even violence from fellow prisoners which, in turn, is likely to lead to your having to be isolated, thereby making the ordeal of incarceration particularly onerous.*

As Sharpe was sentenced he dabbed away tears of self-pity before being led away. John Myles Sharpe, the weak man who felt his wife wore the pants in the family, will be in his 70s before he is eligible for parole. He will have decades to get used to taking orders.